AF333689

OAK

Oak

ONE TREE, THREE YEARS, FIFTY PAINTINGS

Stephen Taylor

With a foreword by Alain de Botton

Princeton Architectural Press

New York

Published by
Princeton Architectural Press
37 East Seventh Street
New York, New York 10003

For a free catalog of books, call 1-800-722-6657.
Visit our website at www.papress.com.

All photographs © author unless otherwise noted.
Ken Adlard, New Moon Photography, Norfolk, UK,
92–93; Iain Lowe, Gerald Sharp Photography,
Essex, UK, 104–5.

All paintings in private collections except those on
pages 46, 52, 54, 75, and 84.

The title of the piece Semipermeable Membrane
and the extract given in the caption on page
83 comes from *Nature Cure* by Richard Mabey,
published by The University of Virginia Press
and in the UK by Chatto and Windus, reprinted
by permission of The Random House Group Ltd.
Copyright © Richard Mabey, 2005.

The Pleasures and Sorrows of Work by Alain de
Botton (Penguin Books, 2009). Copyright © Alain
de Botton, 2009. Reproduced by permission of
Penguin Books Ltd.
United States: From *The Pleasures and Sorrows of
Work* by Alain de Botton, copyright © 2009 by
Alain de Botton. Used by permission of Pantheon
Books, a division of Random House, Inc.
Canada: © Alain de Botton by permission of
United Agents Ltd. (www.unitedagents.co.uk) on
behalf of the author.

Editor: Linda Lee
Designer: Bree Anne Apperley

Special thanks to: Sara Bader,
Nicola Bednarek Brower, Janet Behning,
Fannie Bushin, Megan Carey, Carina Cha,
Tom Cho, Penny (Yuen Pik) Chu, Russell Fernandez,
Jan Haux, Jennifer Lippert, John Myers,
Katharine Myers, Margaret Rogalski,
Dan Simon, Andrew Stepanian, Paul Wagner,
and Joseph Weston of Princeton Architectural
Press —Kevin C. Lippert, publisher

Library of Congress Cataloging-in-Publication
Data

Taylor, Stephen (Stephen Anthony Joseph)
 Oak : one tree, three years, fifty paintings /
Stephen Taylor ; with a foreword by Alain de
Botton. — 1st ed.
     p. cm.
 Includes bibliographical references.
 ISBN 978-1-61689-032-2 (alk. paper)
       1. Taylor, Stephen (Stephen Anthony
Joseph)—Themes, motives. 2. Oak in art. I. Title.
     ND497.T36A4 2011
     759.2—dc23

                                    2011021291

Contents

To my mother and father

Foreword by Alain de Botton

Stephen Taylor has spent much of the last three years in a wheat field in East Anglia repeatedly painting the same oak tree under a range of different lights and weathers. He was out in two feet of snow last winter, and this summer, at three in the morning, he lay on his back tracing the upper branches of the tree by the light of a solstice moon.

On a typical summer's day, this little-known middle-aged artist is loading his car, ready for work, by seven in the morning. He lives in an old terraced house in the centre of Colchester, a town of one hundred thousand inhabitants, ninety kilometres northeast of London. His Citroën has reached a stage of decrepitude so advanced that it seems set for immortality. Across the back seats, strewn as if the vehicle had just been involved in a head-on collision, are canvases, easels, insect repellent, old sandwiches, a bag of brushes, and a box of paints. There is also a suitcase jammed with scarves and jumpers, for outdoor painters tend to know the story of how Cézanne caught a chill one morning while painting a sparrow in a field in Aix-en-Provence—and was dead by sunset.

The road out of Colchester leads Taylor past a fractured landscape of warehouses and building sites. The commuter traffic is impatient and quick to anger. Near the train station, an old crab-apple tree stands in the middle of a roundabout, an unlikely survivor of the roadwork that made off with its fellows. Eight miles north of town, Taylor turns off the main road and starts down a little-used farm track. Waist-high stalks bow and disappear beneath the front bumper, like hair through a comb. Taylor finds his usual parking place and, fifteen metres from the tree, arranges his base camp in a clearing in the wheat.

The oak is estimated to be 250 years old. It was therefore already home to skylarks and starlings when Jane Austen was a baby and George III the ruler of the American colonies.

To those familiar with paintings as polished, fully realised objects hanging in museums, it comes as a surprise to see the sheer mass of bulky, soiled equipment required for their creation. Taylor has more than a hundred species of brushes including hog's hair ones with filbert tips, sable points, round heads, shaving brushes, soft Japanese watercolour brushes, and handmade badger blenders.

Next to these, Taylor sets down a no less heterogeneous assortment of gnarled tubes of paint, which together make up his visual alphabet. It is hard to believe that these ingredients could be combined to create meticulously detailed skylarks, spring leaves, and lichen-coated branches. Pastes that in lesser hands would end up as mud will be tamed and recast to take on the guise of facets of the earth and sky.

In time there will be no reminders of the fleshly origins of painting. The dark magenta stains on the artist's fingers, the red speckles on his shoes, the glutinous green and blue smears on his palettes—all of these will be dissolved away, leaving the paintings to stand by themselves, as silent about their material parentage as a newly laid-out country road. To watch Taylor at work is to be reminded that even Perugino and Mantegna, prone to be mentioned only as disembodied names in histories of European art, were once corporeal beings who dabbed paint onto bits of wood using sticks tipped with pig's bristles, and at the end of the day returned home from their studios with fingernails stained by the tints they had used to fashion the cottony clouds that float serenely above the heads of their infant Christs.

Taylor sets to work on the lower left-hand branches of a tree study he began a week ago. Between thumb and forefinger, he manipulates a sable brush, dipping its tip into a tear of magenta and raw sienna oil, which will later, seen from a distance, coagulate into a perfect implication of a leaf in the noonday sun. Two hawks fly high above the field, on the lookout for rabbits stirring in the wheat.

Introduction:
Why Paint an Oak Tree?

I grew up surrounded by oak trees. The sun rose in the east over the English West Midlands, passed over our house and garden, and set to the west between the houses across the road, over the hills of Shropshire and far-off Wales. Our suburb was built in the 1940s, a world of avenues, lawns, hedges, and small vegetable plots. We all walked or cycled to school, past oak trees left over from woods and fields not quite obliterated by our generally happy way of life. Figure 1

Everywhere we went there were oaks: outside my primary school (and on my school cap), on the shore of the fishing lake, and lit up by orange street light as we left the pub at closing time. These oaks were familiar. But I'd almost forgotten them when, much later and as an almost different man, I decided to look at one for three years at the edge of a field on the east side of England. Figures 2–5

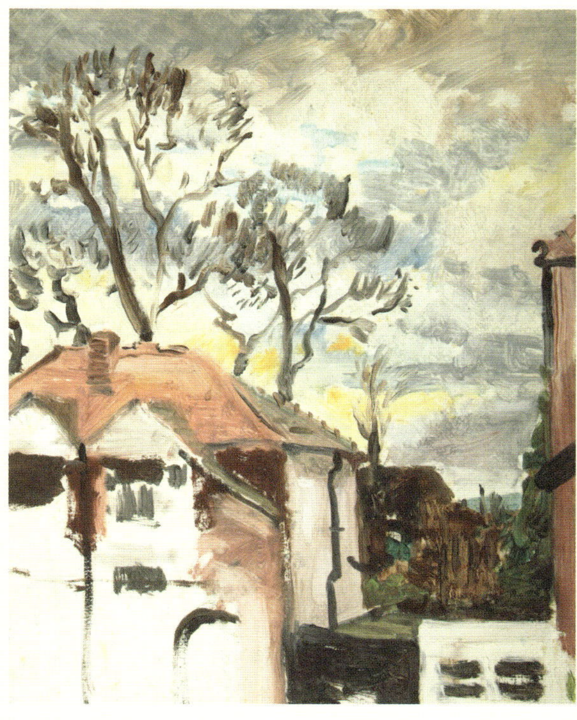

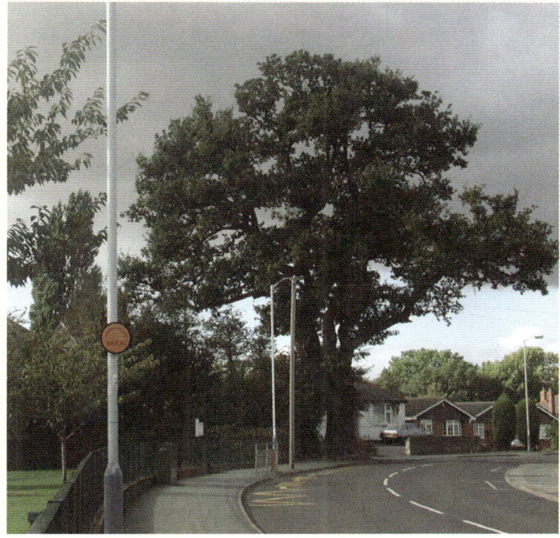

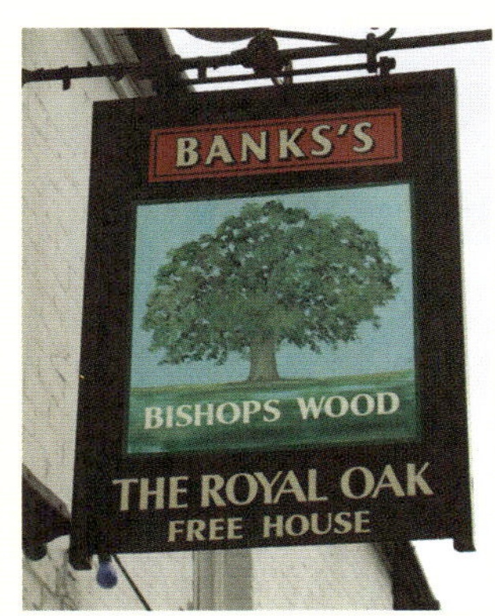

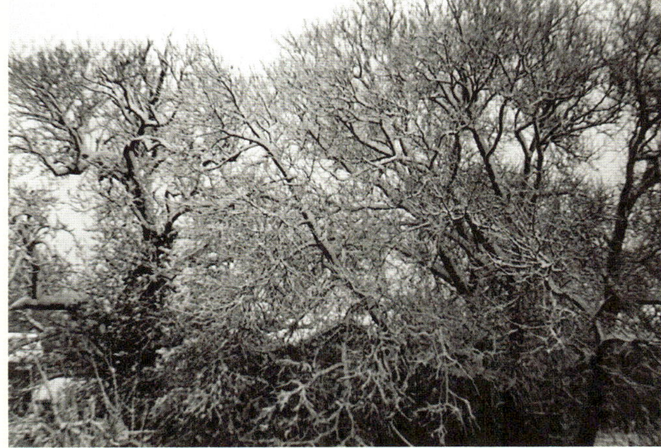

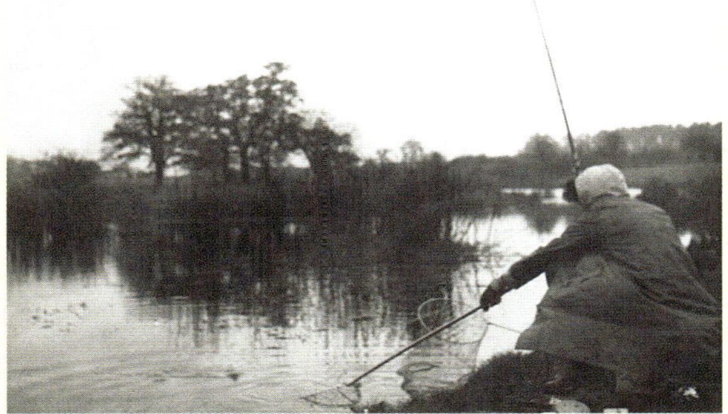

Clockwise from top left:
1 | *Oaks during Sunset*. Oil on board, 280 mm x 210 mm. A painting of a view from a front bedroom in my childhood home, made when I was sixteen.
2 | A huge oak by the gate of my primary school. I didn't know it was an oak at the time. It was just a tree that the footpath carefully snakes around. When I was small I don't think I liked it very much; but it was always there.
3 | Oak and willow in snow at the bottom of our garden, photographed from my bedroom window as a teenager
4 | Me at fourteen, with oaks in the background
5 | A sign outside a pub not far from where I grew up. King Charles II hid in a nearby oak tree to escape the forces of Parliament after the battle of Worcester in 1651.

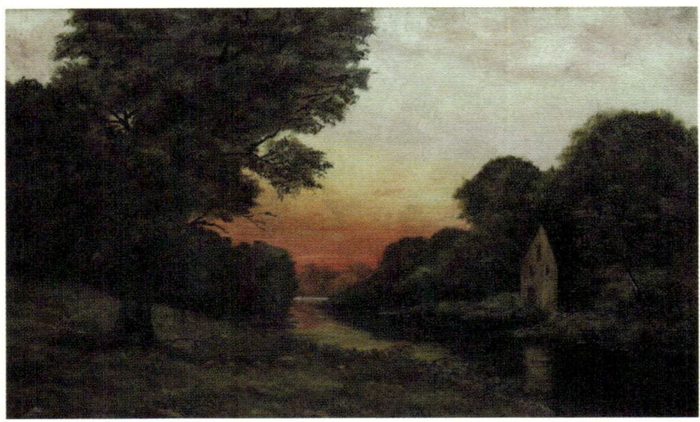

6|Jack Taylor, *Sunset with Oak Tree*, 1928. Oil on canvas, 360 mm x 240 mm. My grandfather's picture has the generalised features of a formulaic European landscape painting, but it is close to reality. The wooded valley faces west to the sunset, exactly like the valley in which he was living at the time; the valley still has a canal and a stream. My family shares a memory of grandfather taking his paints and easel down there.

I grew up with painting. My school books were full of drawings and paintings, especially for geography and biology; and my art teacher helped to develop my skill. There were paintings on the walls of the homes where I lived in and in those I visited. And some of them had been hanging there a long time.

My grandfather, Jack Taylor, was a brewery clerk, and like many working men, he was interested in art and at weekends found time to paint. In 1928 he made an oil painting of a landscape with an oak tree, which now hangs on the wall of my cousin's study. Figures 6 and 7 The walls of our own dining room had two waterfall paintings by grandfather as well as watercolours of birds by my father, a postman.

However, I took this tradition of art and developed a new, deliberate approach by going to art school. In fact, I became super aware of art and its cultural meanings because I attended academic universities, not a craft-based school. I was taught to analyse art, write about it, and to argue a position. I began working toward a doctorate on technique and perception in the work of John Constable.

Painting trees wasn't on the curriculum, but we covered history and theory. But more important to me was that I was able to apprentice during this time with a visiting tutor and one of the best observational painters in the country, Paul Gopal-Chowdhury. It was a huge stroke of luck. Through him I was able to refine the observation-based painting I already knew and get the continuity of practice that you need to develop any craft. My work became more sophisticated and analytical, and I began selling paintings before I left university. Figure 8

After graduating I took a job as a resident artist at a boarding school in Essex and didn't finish my PhD. I did a lot of lecturing. I had a career plan: I would be an artist and work on commission, meet people from all walks of life, and have a good time, improving my technique but without the objective of getting rich or famous. And this, more or less, was what happened.

Then, in my late thirties, life took a nasty turn. My mother died of a brain tumour, very slowly. A few years later someone I loved, and who had been the closest woman to me after my mother, died of the same disease. Around this time my father had a stroke, and I was going back

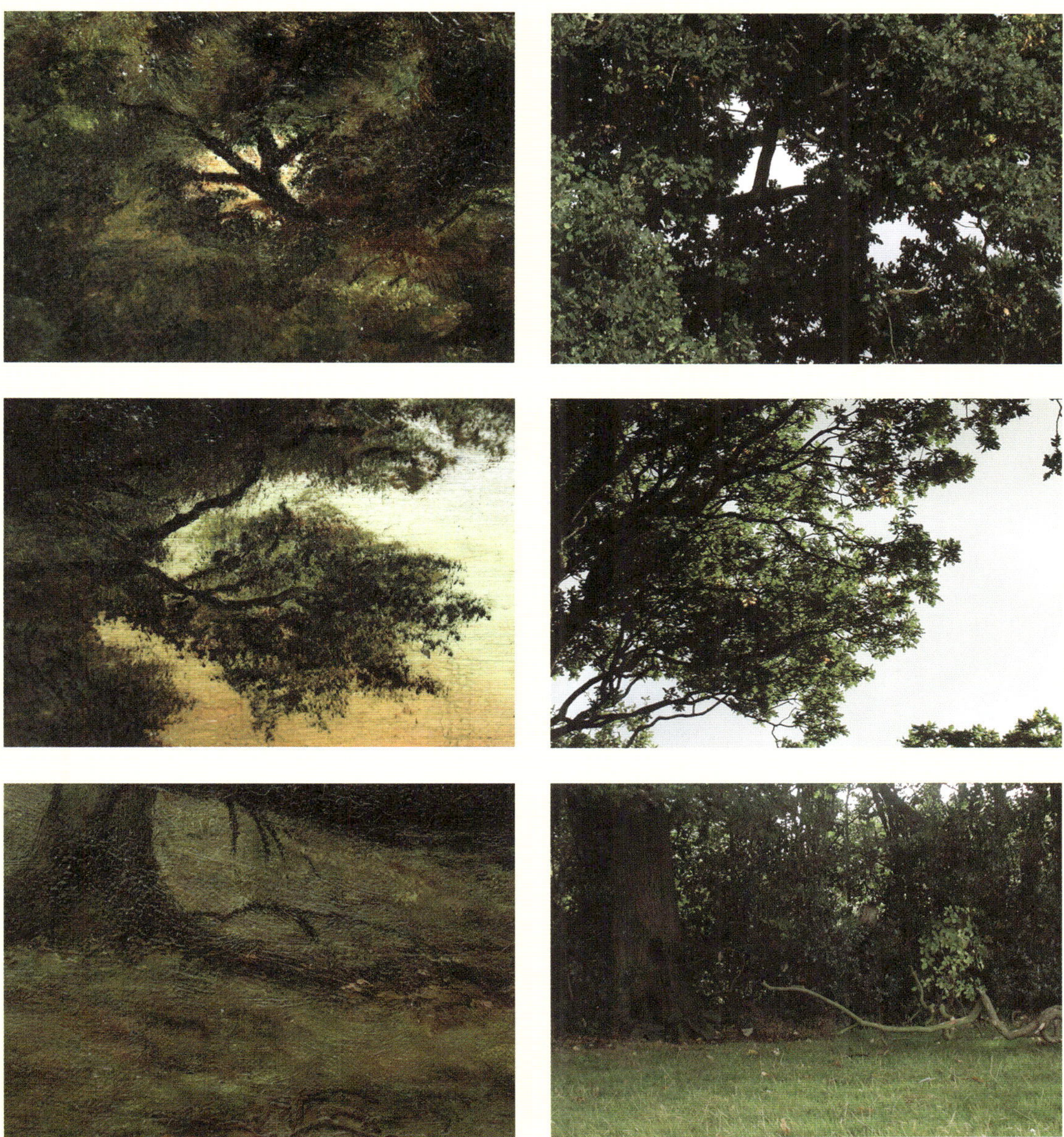

7 | The oak tree is full of details that may be missed if not looked at carefully. The three photographs that I took (on the right), which mirror parts of *Sunset with Oak Tree*, reveal this: inside the foliage there is a silhouette of branches against the sky; sunlight filters through some leaves but not others; and fallen branches litter the ground. These features of the painted tree are a bit disjointed, but if you add your own observations to a pattern, this is what can happen.

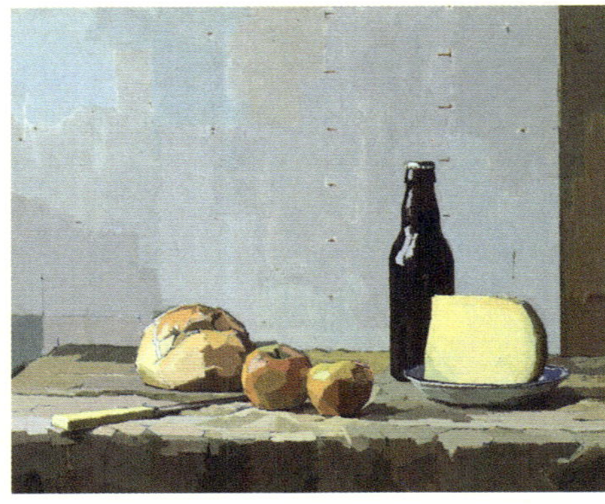

8 | *Bread, Beer, Apples and Cheese*. Oil on canvas, 360 mm x 290 mm. The first painting I sold at university, which was bought by a friend for her parents and is now in their kitchen.

home more frequently. We became very close, but he died not long after. I found myself sitting in my childhood home, not quite knowing where I was.

PAINTING AS A TORCH

Painting was a constant in my life. When I returned to Essex, I decided to work for myself. The first topics I approached were old stories of death and rebirth. I taught myself some anatomy and painted Christ in the tomb. Then a crucifixion. Then a female crucifixion. I travelled to Sicily looking for the site where Persephone had descended into the underworld.

I was still looking for subjects when friends from New Zealand rang me out of the blue and invited me to a farm they had just bought, a short distance from where I was living. The house was old and big; there was a pool and eight hundred acres of North Essex farmland, only a few miles from where Constable had worked two hundred years before.

At about the time of this visit, I realised something was missing in my new paintings, a constant from my childhood life—the countryside. Of my own work my favourite pieces were usually landscapes. I asked my friends if I could paint on the farm. They said yes, and I worked there for seven years.

DAYLIGHT AND MOONLIGHT

I discovered a field sloping gently south to a small stream with willow trees. Low hedges ran along its other three sides, and from the northeast corner I could see the whole field laid out in front of me beneath a low horizon of distant fields and trees—an ordinary Essex country scene. Painting from here, the sun and moon would rise on my left and set to my right. I would be undisturbed and free to come and go as I pleased.

Over the next four years, I put together—just of work with this field as the subject— an exhibition for the Arts Centre at King's College, Cambridge. It was a journey that explored a single location, and it helped me to recover a sense of where I was in life. I drew from the tradition that I felt most strongly about, of observed landscape, but I wanted to show that landscape painting—nature painting—could be modern. I would make six-feet-wide paintings like Constable, but they would be new. I began to work on ways that would help me paint nature in a fresh way and to help me make visual contact with this new place.

I made different visual maps of what I saw. I plotted small changes of height on the horizon from contours of an Ordinance Survey map. I used the base of clouds to create a perspective grid in the sky, and I painted the crop as a texture gradient. For elusive, changing colours, I devised a method of colour mapping using observed, painted colours and digital images. (See pages 94–101, in "From Start to Finish: Making an Oak Tree Painting.") Figure 9

In all these endeavours, I embraced as much science as I could. I spoke to scientist friends and found ways to use science to help me to see more clearly.[1] And I now believe I was drawing on the knowledge I had learnt at school: that visual images can explain as well as captivate.

FINDING THE OAK

As soon as the exhibition was up at King's College, I felt a sense of achievement but also felt it had failed in some ways. I certainly had a sense of place, and I had shared it with others. But I had not created a sense of how thousands of smaller worlds exist within a panorama—each with its own character.

I wanted the next show to expand on what could be found in this field, and I wanted my painting style to develop. By being in the field so often and by working so carefully in colours belonging to particular conditions, I had developed an understanding of the limitlessness of natural colour. Every time I now walked across the field, the colour world felt different. Perhaps I could make the next step by thinking about the new understanding of painting that had grown while working on this show.

I went back to the field.

Over the next few months, I spent time bird watching and was outdoors in every kind of weather. I took a lot of photographs and made sketches and small oil studies. There was an oak, just behind

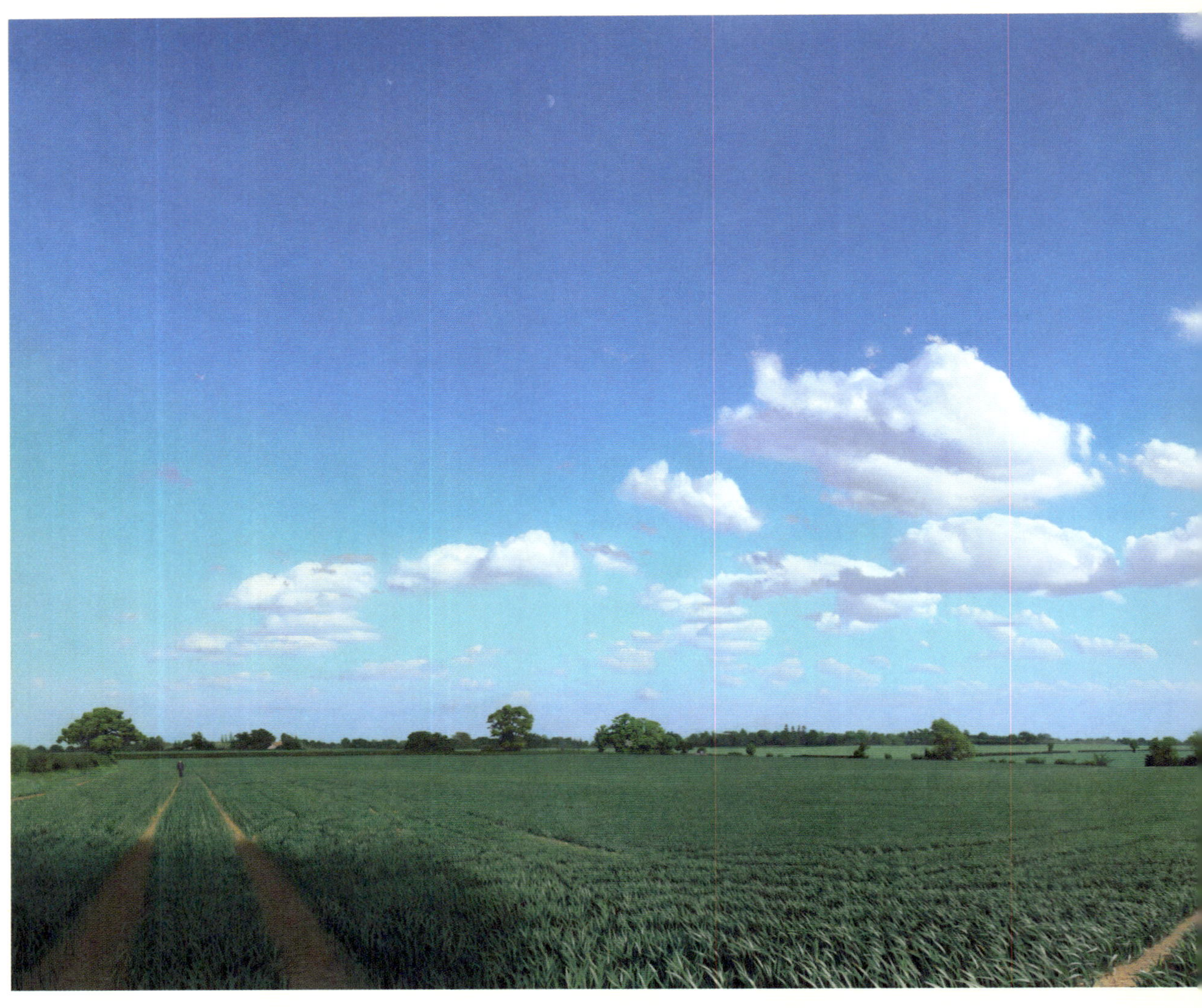

9 | *Spring, West Bergholt, England.* Oil on board,
1830 mm x 910 mm. An agronomist who saw
this painting commented, "Everything I see in
that field, I see here."

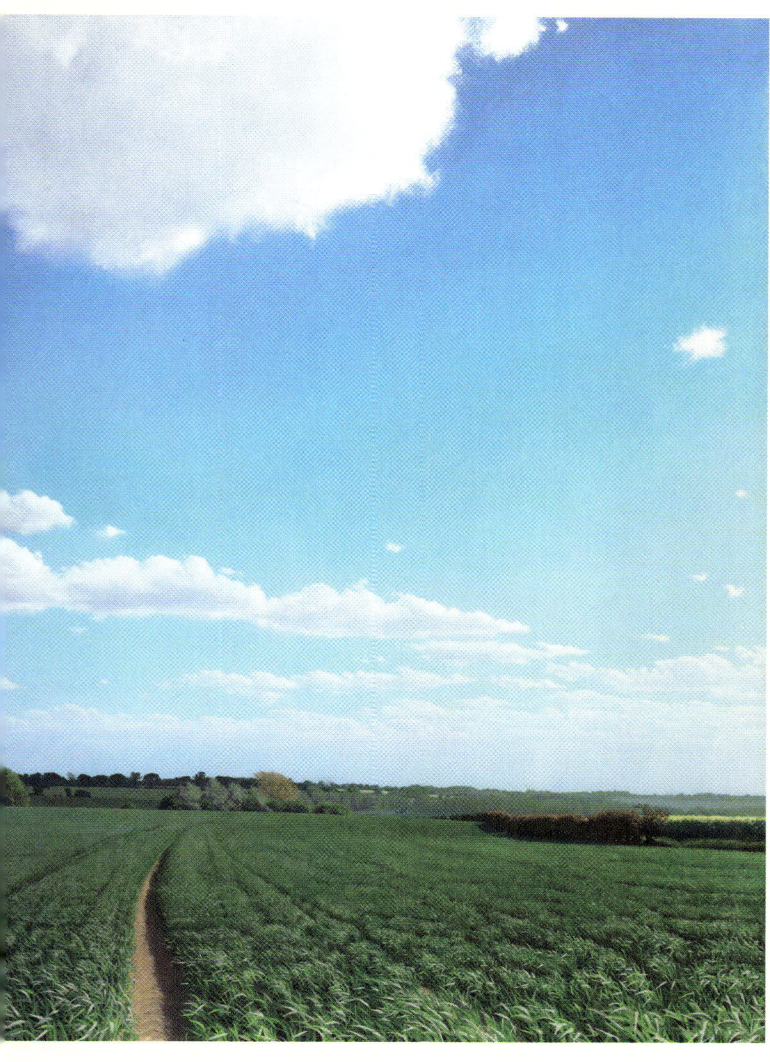

Below, left to right:
10 | *Spring, West Bergholt, England*, detail.
I briefly considered a show with the willow tree as the subject. When I was a child, there was a huge willow at the foot of our garden, and I could remember the feel of its bark. Willows have subtle green-greys that catch the light. Unfortunately, this one was later cut down to make cricket bats!
11 | *Spring, West Bergholt, England*, detail. There were also oak trees in the field. This one in the north hedge might have been a good subject if it hadn't looked like an umbrella—it was the wrong shape for me.
12 | *Spring, West Bergholt, England*, detail. A promising oak on the eastern hedge.

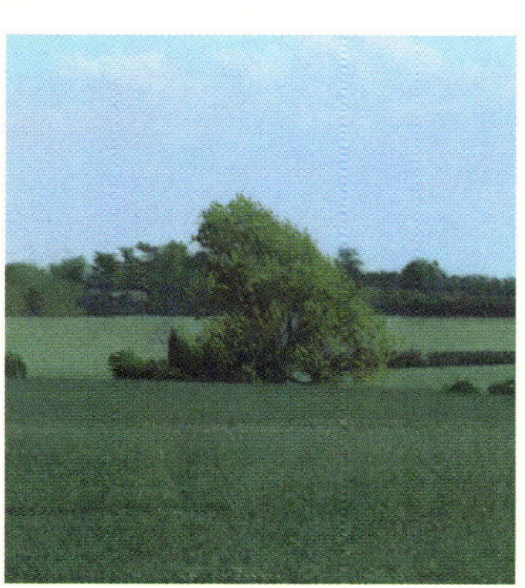

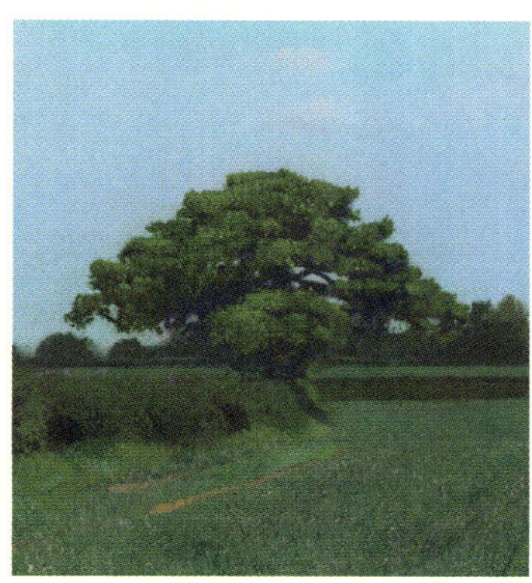

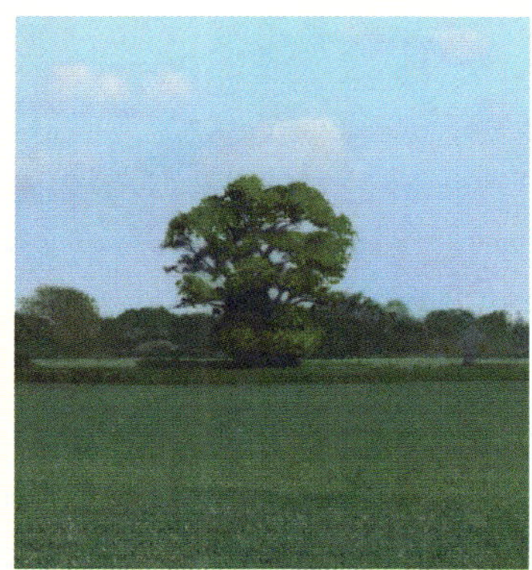

a hedge on the eastern side, that looked particularly promising. The branches from the lower part of the trunk had been pollarded (cut back), so its upper part seemed to float. From the field in winter, it had a dramatic, clear structure against the sky. In summer, it was a magnet for birds, and as the sun crossed the sky it reflected sunlight in such a way that you did not see its shaded side, making the tree look quite flat. The whole thing lit up like a colour-changing emblem. Figures 10–12

I made the first painting during a June afternoon in 2003 (and the last one in August of 2006), sitting in a rape crop when the seed pods were a lurid pale green. I have an aversion to the smell of rape, so perhaps I was more aware than usual of the alien aspect of a modern field, with its manufactured crop imposed onto the land. The incredible energy you can sense in a field packed with a single crop seemed to seep into the tree.

The result was something different from the paintings in the first show. This tree is not an element in a panorama but something made from interactions between colours and textures, as well as my own interaction with the tree. Figure 13 It is a "wet on wet" painting. Painting oil on top of wet oil means that it is difficult to separate and easy to destroy colour mixes. To avoid this I paint fairly thickly and very decisively. This forces your hand, and for some reason, when you work fast, marks can easily take on a rhythm of their own. But if you look at the subject carefully, fiercely even, and take *its* visual patterns, you can make one rhythm "surf" the other. You go with the flow but cut your own line.

I took the image home and put it up in the studio. Over the next few months, I completed more studies and took more photos in the field—day and night—looking for something to develop. But I kept coming back to the oak tree.

Reflecting back on it, the contrast between commercial crop and solitary tree was what looked promising. And the exclusion of everything in the landscape but tree, sky, and crop had a condensing effect. It also resulted in a composition in three time dimensions: a slowly changing tree, a more quickly changing crop, and rapidly changing weather and light. Each scale of time seemed to play off the others.

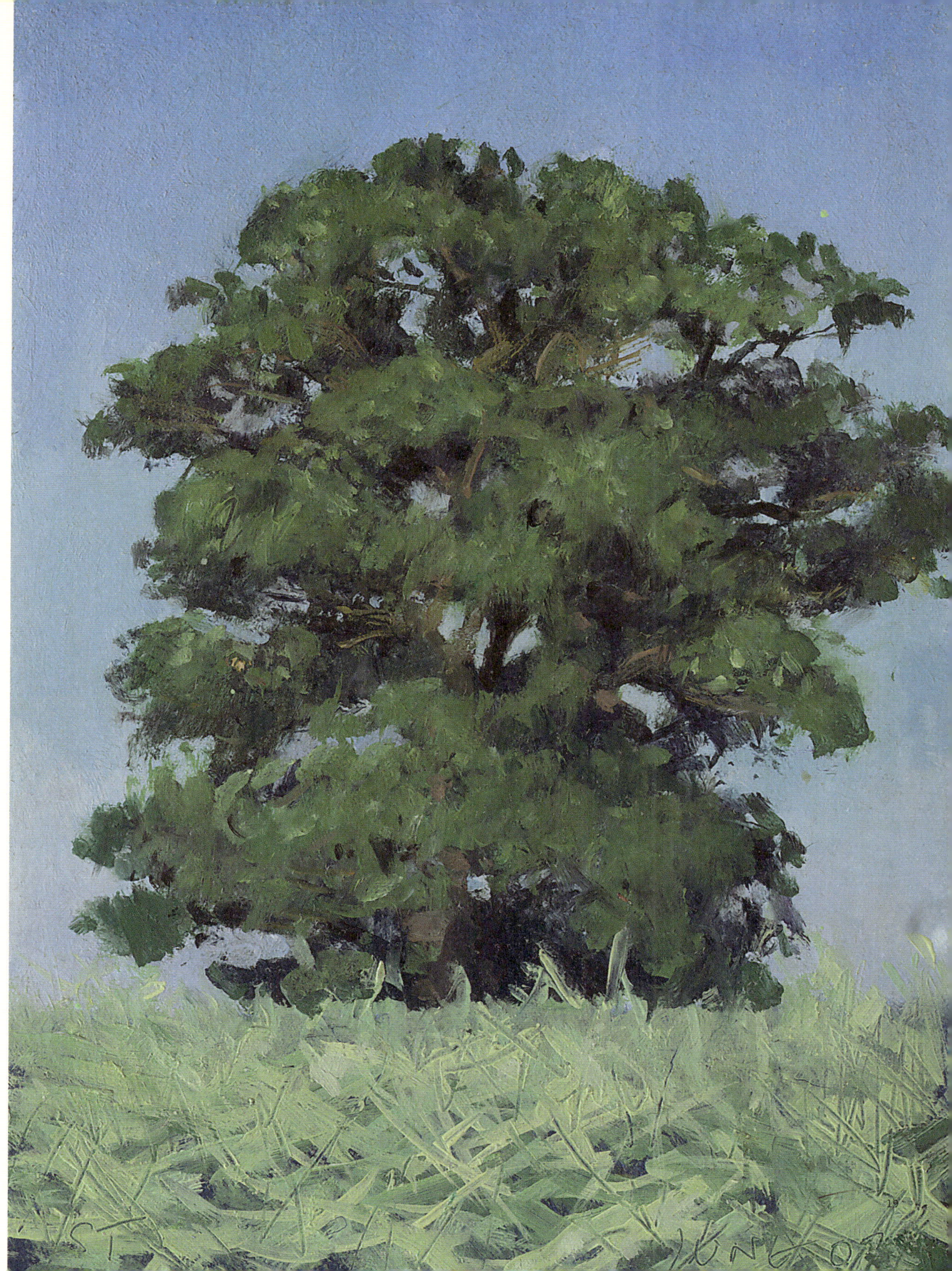

In October I did another series of studies. The oak had now shed leaves, and from fifty metres those remaining looked like a haze of sienna and orange pin pricks. More branches were visible than before, now black-red against a turquoise sky. What I saw made me decide to work "wet on dry," painting an oil layer mixed with cobalt drier to accelerate drying overnight. I would then go back during similar weather conditions to add more colours, typically for five or six sessions. The inconvenience is compensated for by clarity and purity of colour, and better control over edges and textures. This technique allowed me to paint the orange dots of the leaves and the pattern of branches inside the sky. Figure 14

When this oak was finished, I found a surprise. I had not expected to see that, when placed next to each other, each oak study would look so distinct that they appeared to be different trees. They made me think about the ways in which they *were* the same tree.

The range of colour and textures in the field was also striking. The rape had been harvested, and the ground sown with winter wheat. The crop-rotation sequence on the farm was usually rape to wheat to barley, so during different times over the three years, there would be three crops at different stages of development.

Each element seemed to contribute something different from the landscape. The crop was man made. The hedge was a threshold. The sky was above everything and would change. And the oak stood as a symbol of nature and of place. But these oak paintings would not be based on preconceived ideas about oaks. They would be discovered by looking and painting. Figure 15

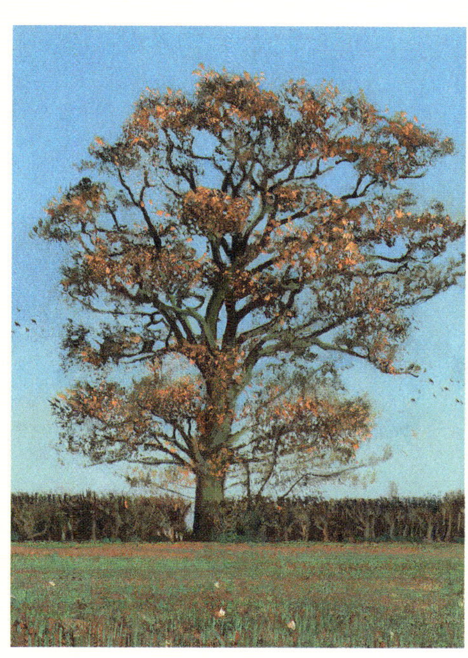

14 | *Flints*. Oil on board, 183 mm x 130 mm.
Seconc oak tree painting, wet on dry.
15 | The tree photographed from a glider 300
metres above

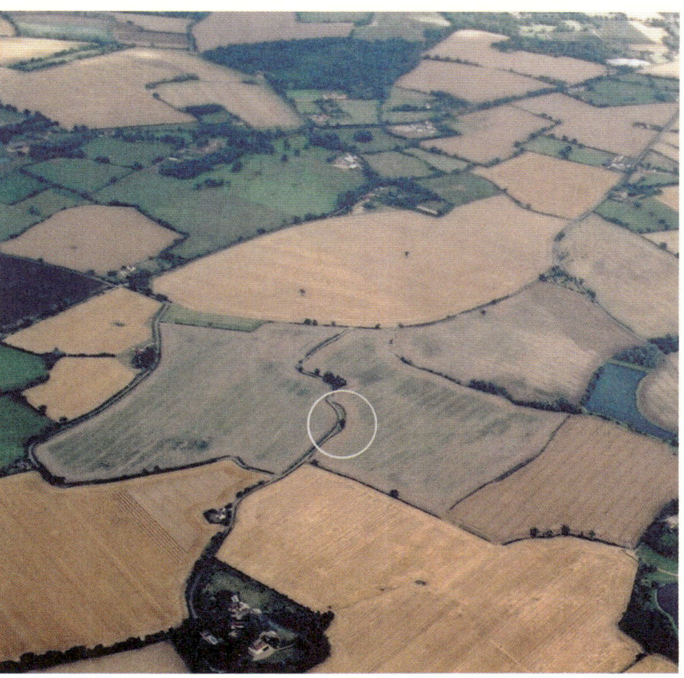

Plates

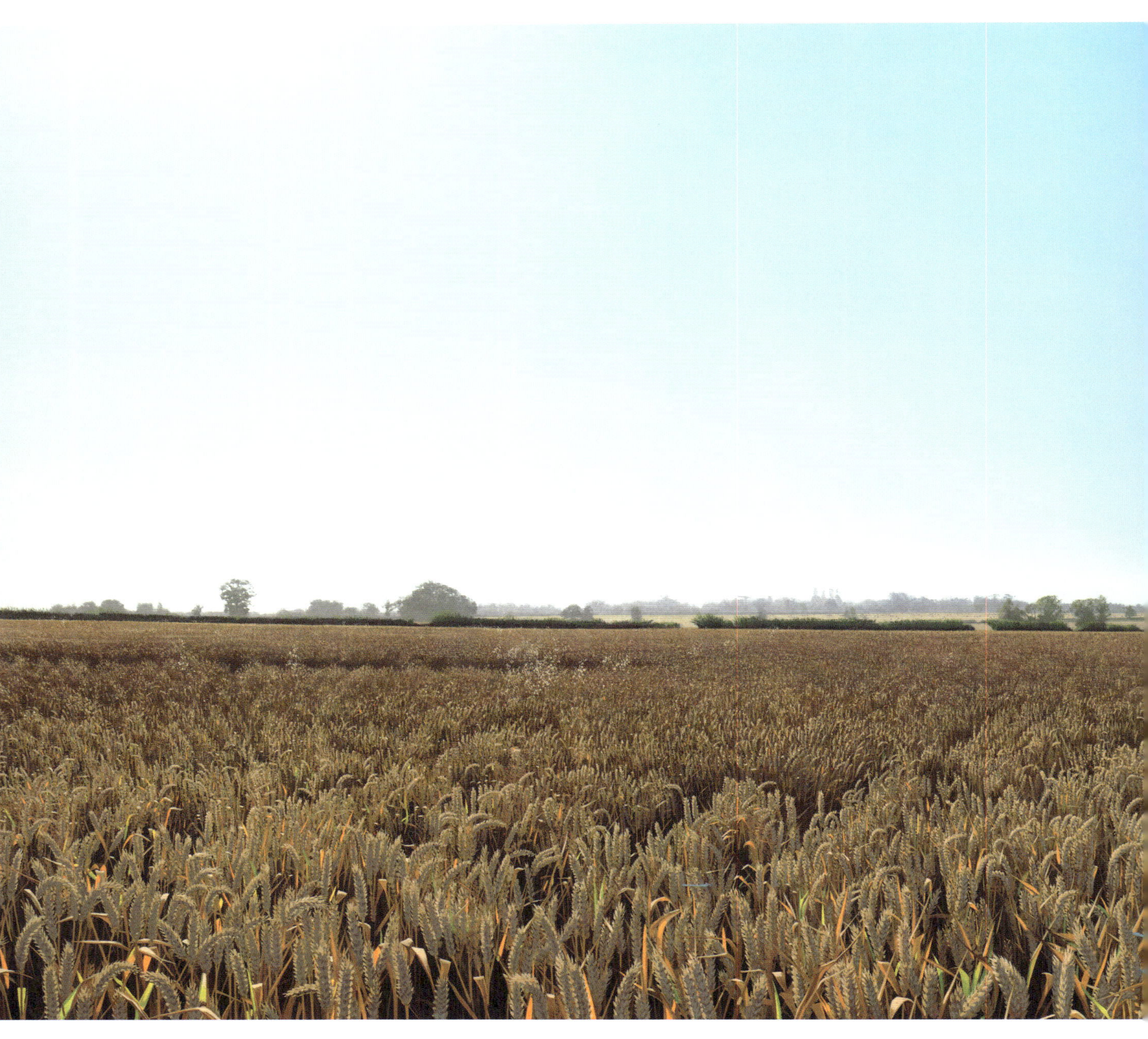

Summer, West Bergholt, England. Oil on canvas, 1910 mm x 810 mm.

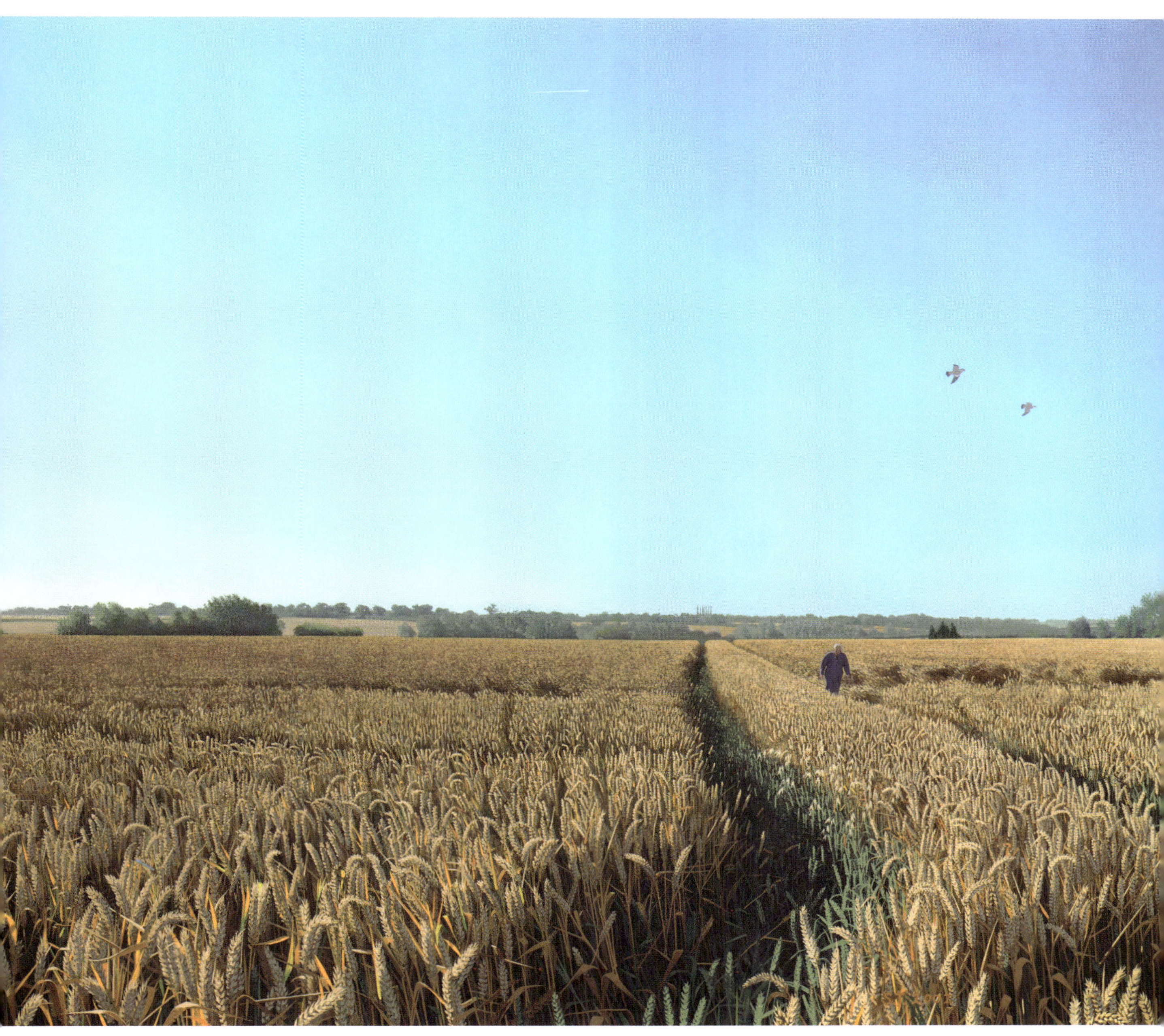

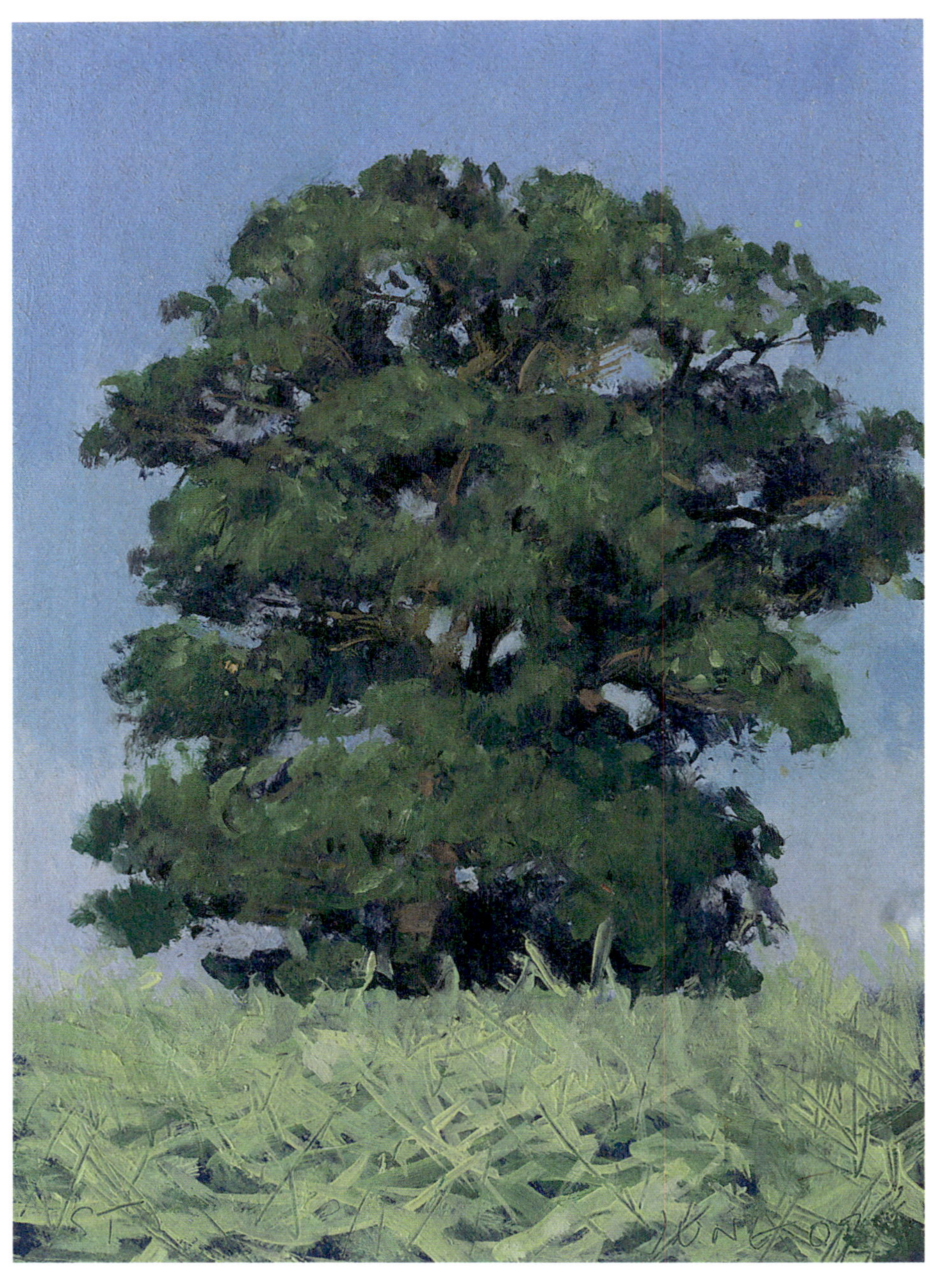

Green Fire. Oil on board, 183 mm x 130 mm.

The title originates in a memory from when I was seventeen.

I was at the local cinema watching a film about the English Civil War. During a scene of a cavalry charge, when a horse leapt over a wall of pikes, something snapped inside me. I walked out of the cinema and toward the countryside, feeling upset and inconsolable. What I saw in the fields was not hedges and trees but green fire. Everything was transformed, and I felt unspeakable relief. I fell asleep right there, and when I awoke I was under an oak tree, looking up.

This experience recalled the poetry of Thomas Traherne and the music of composers like Gerald Finzi and Ralph Vaughan Williams—and I see something like it in the personal correspondence of John Constable. The most important thing these artists have in common is that they take intensely private experiences of the landscape—nature through the senses— and turn them into something that can be shared by others.

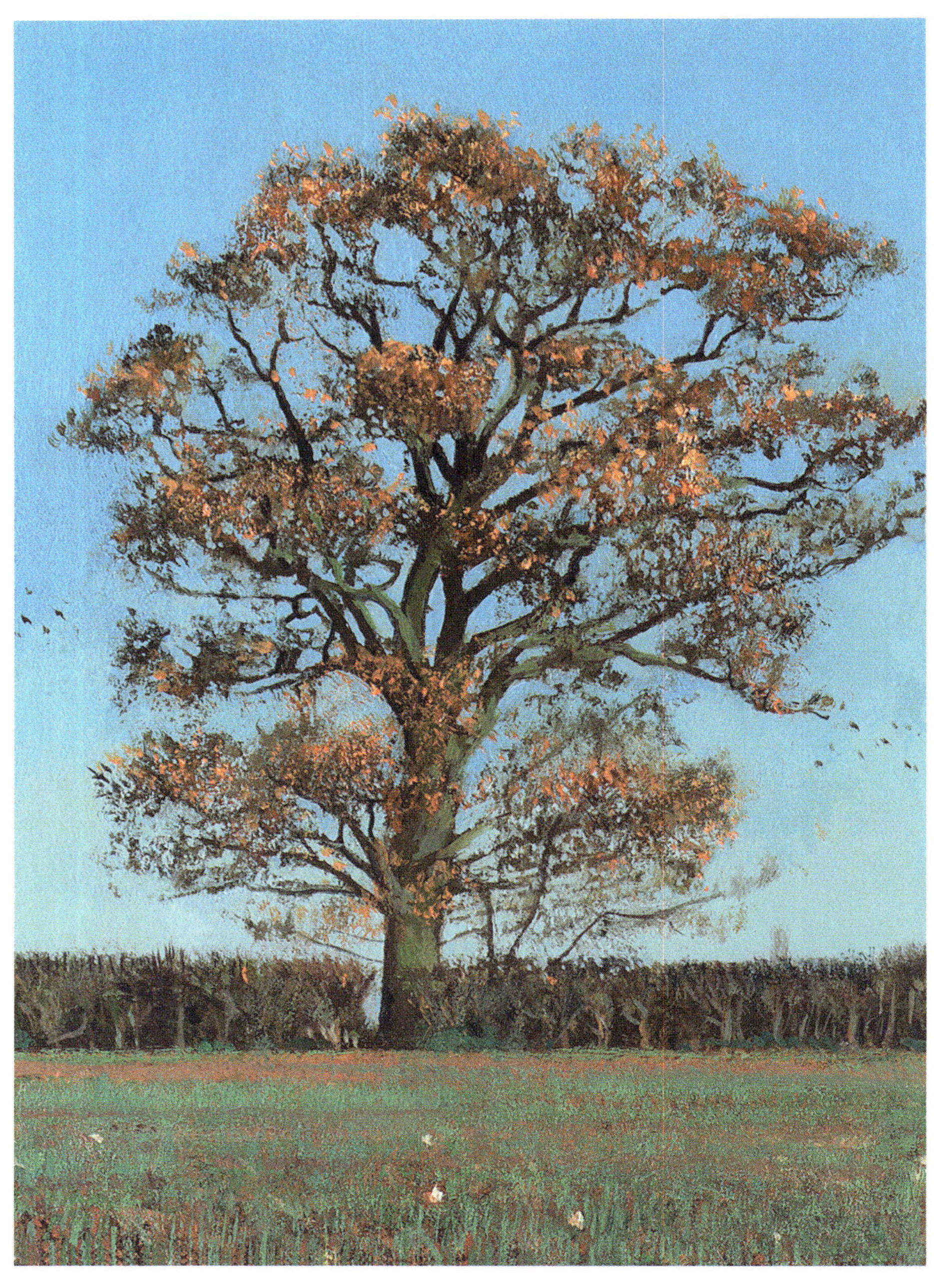

Flints. Oil on board, 183 mm x 130 mm.

The field has been sown with winter wheat, which already shows green
shoots. Rape helps improve the yield of the cereal crop that follows.
Wheat, which needs plenty of nutrients, follows rape in the crop rotation.

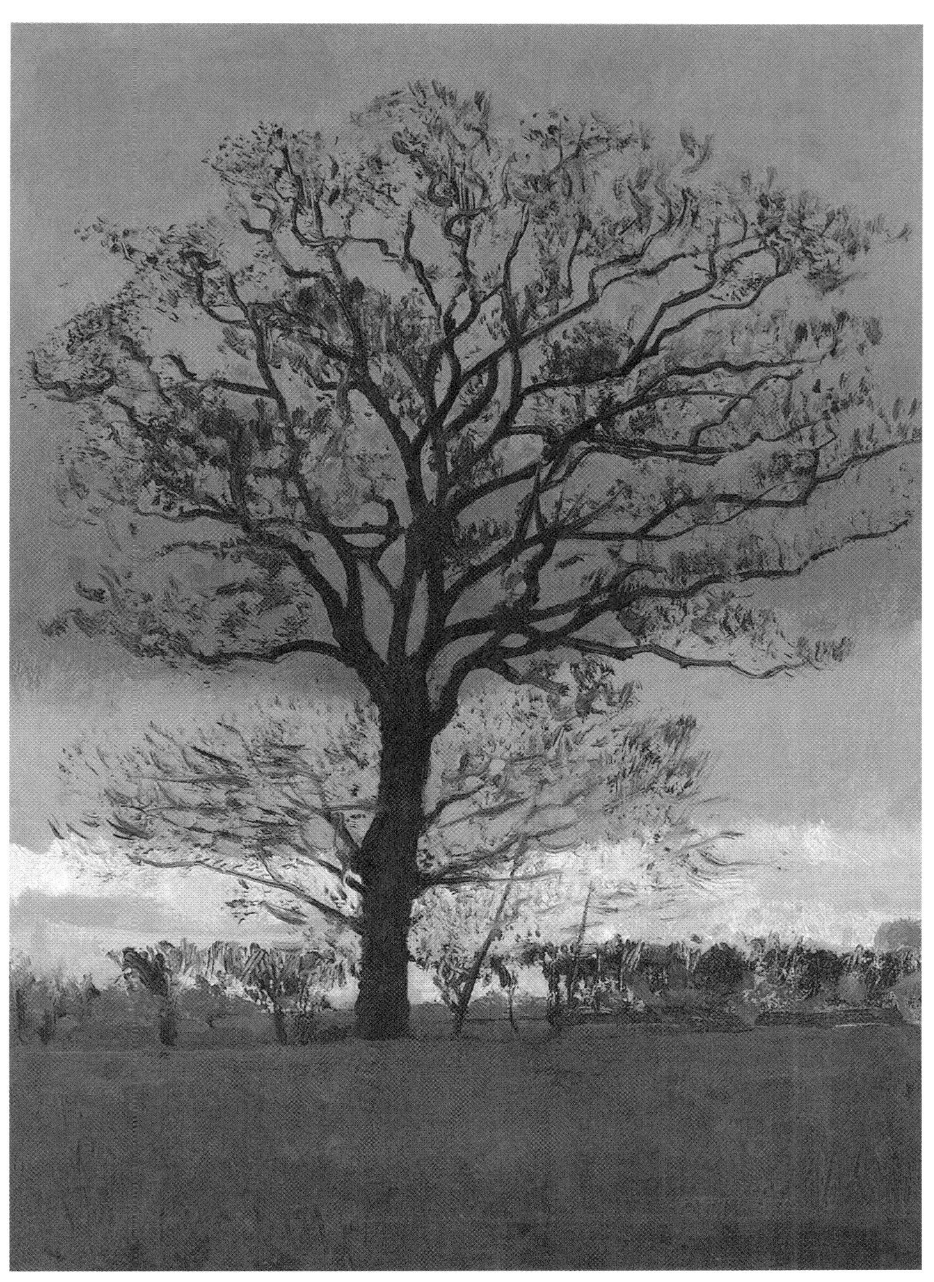

Elm Sapling. Oil on board, 183 mm x 130 mm.

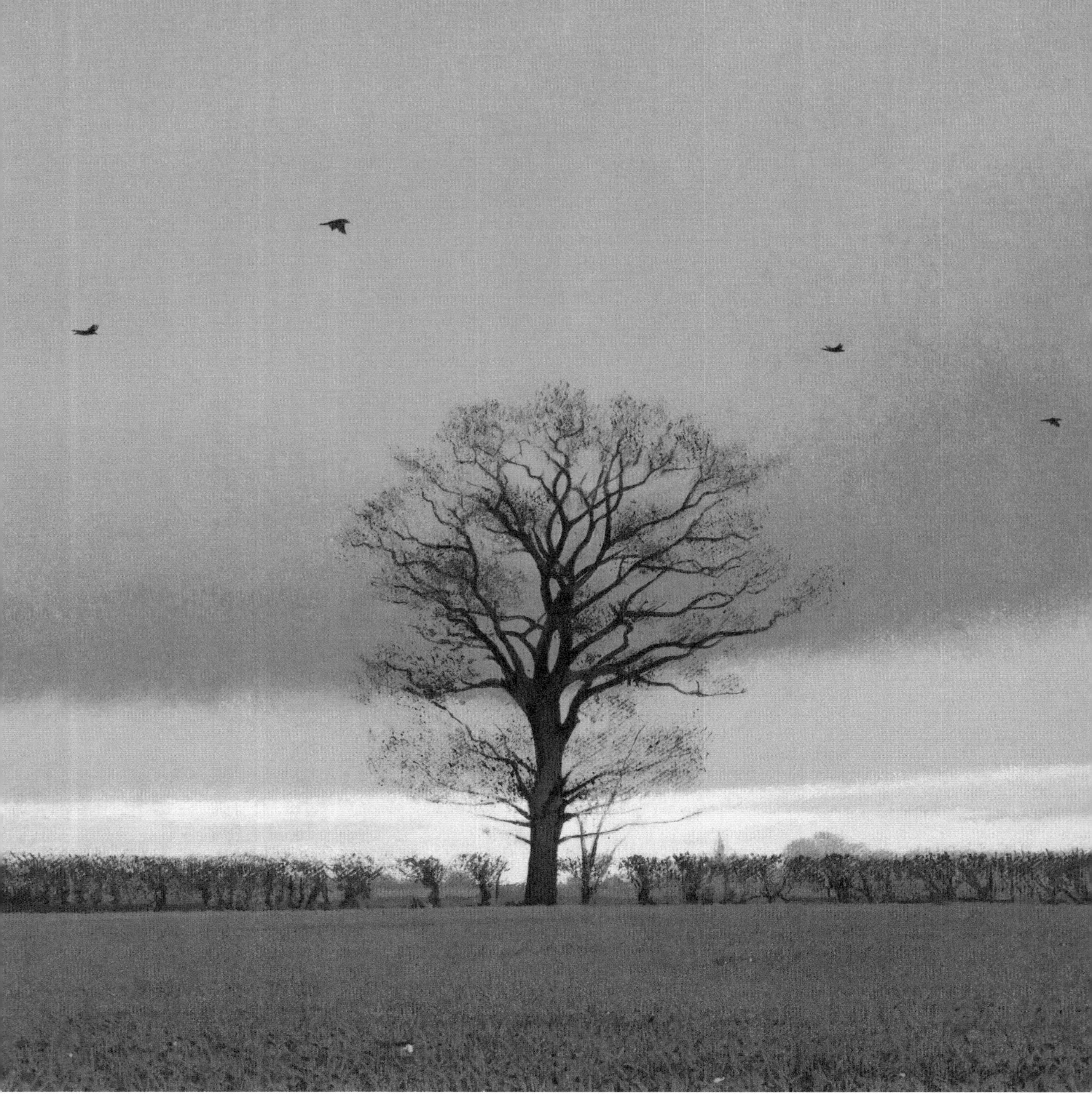

Oak and Crows. Oil on board, 300 mm x 300 mm.

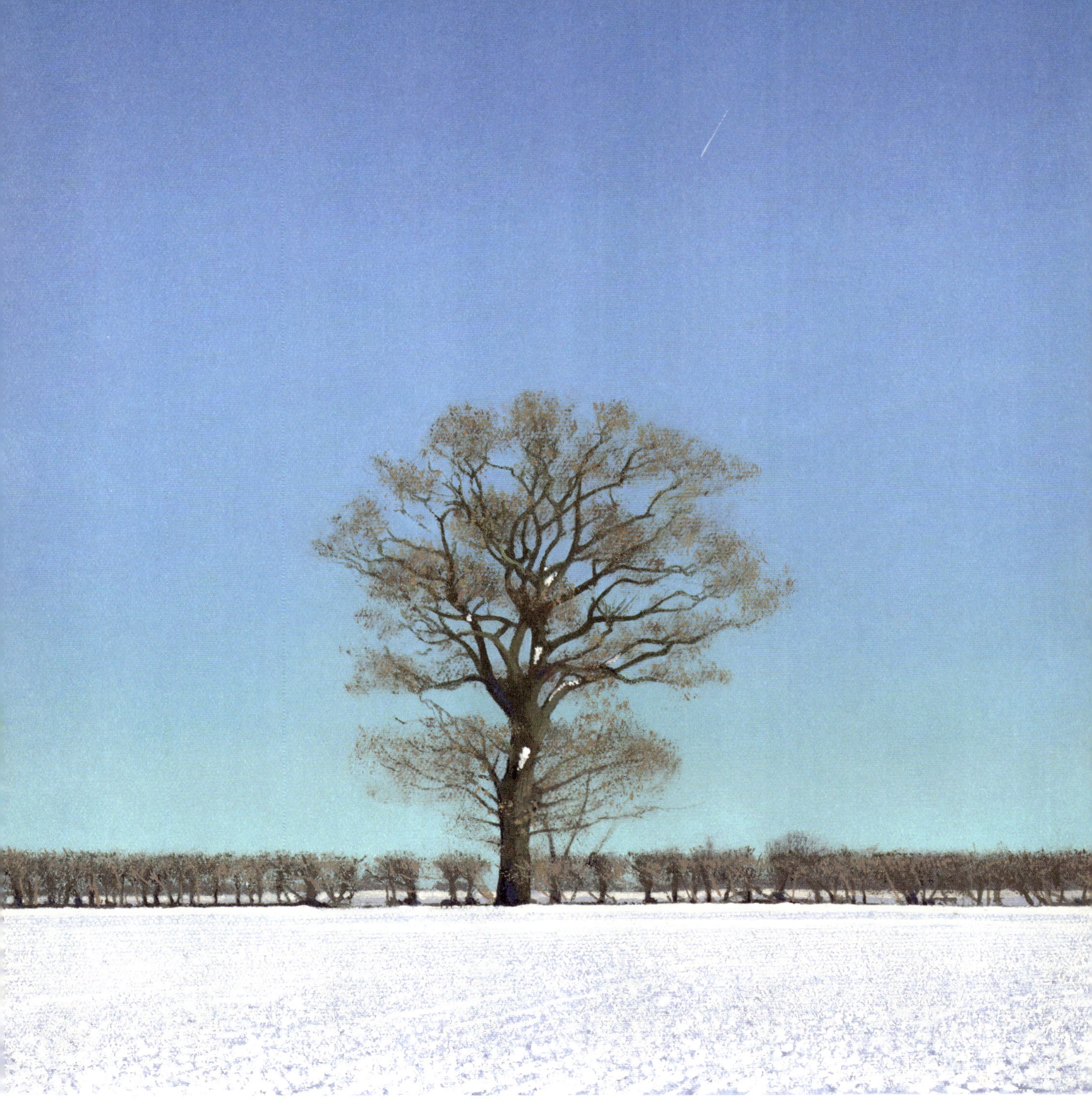

Oak after Snow. Oil on canvas, 300 mm x 300 mm.

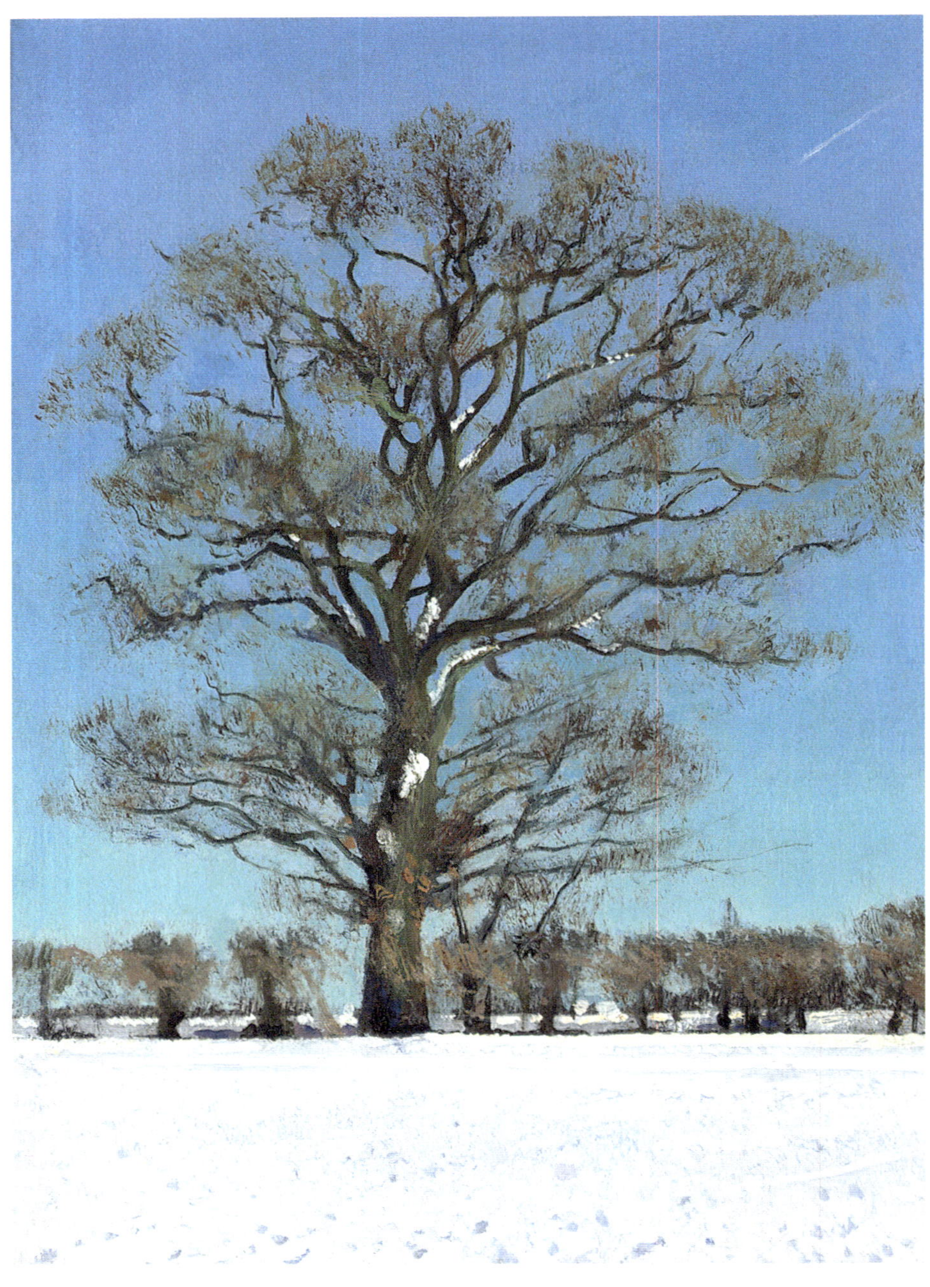

High-altitude Jet. Oil on board, 183 mm x 130 mm.

During the three winters I worked with the oak tree, barely an inch or two of snow fell, and it quickly melted. When it did snow, I got to the site as quickly as possible. I need at least three days of similar weather to finish a small painting like this. If not, I might have to jump in the car months later at the slightest sign of snow in the hope of finishing the painting.

Setting up in snow on a clear winter day is blissful. There's an endless white carpet that is full of interesting unevenness: hairs of winter wheat prick through thin snow, little black holes, blue-violet shadows, and crystals—billions of crystals.

In bright weather, contrast effects are easily visible. For example, if you look at the faintly yellow highlights of snow then at a dark tree trunk, the trunk momentarily seems blue—a contrast effect. If you look back at the snow and peer into its shadows, a blue-violet light appears. The sky is equally colourful: overhead is ultramarine with a red undertone, the horizon a neon turquoise. Dramatic, stark, and alive, the colours challenge you.

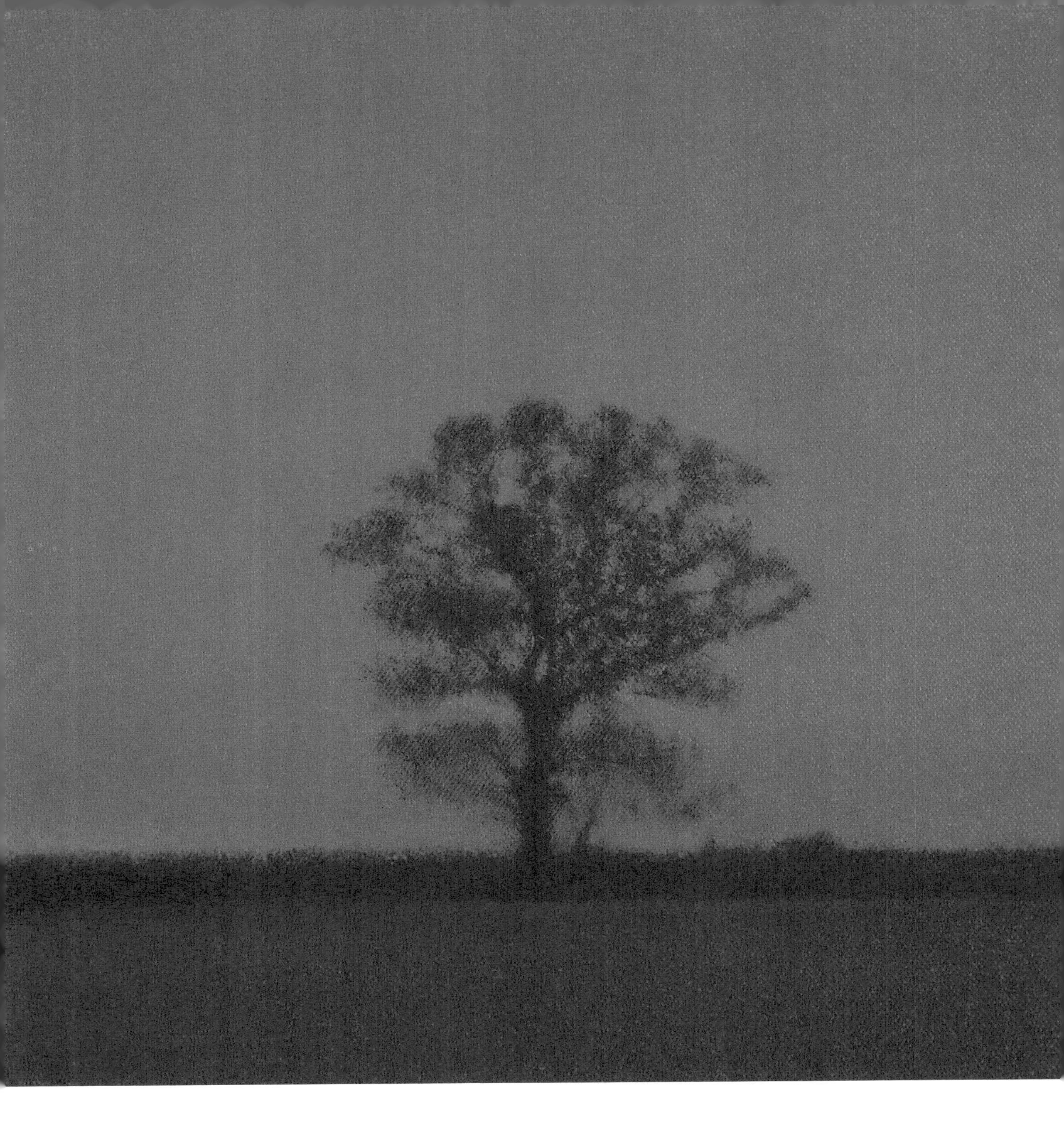

Oak at Night in Winter. Oil on canvas, 300 mm x 300 mm.

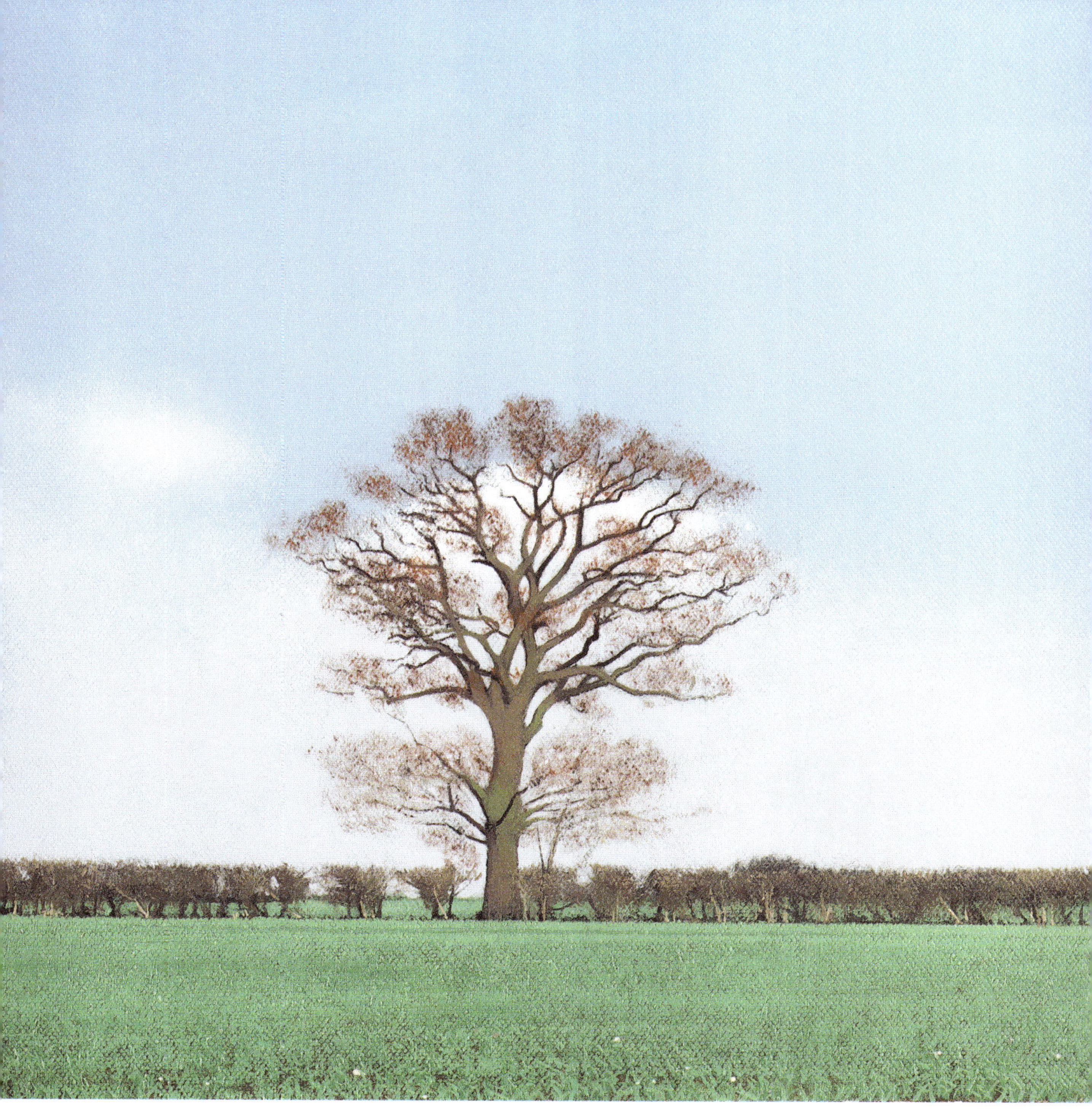

Oak in Early Spring. Oil on canvas, 300 mm x 300 mm.

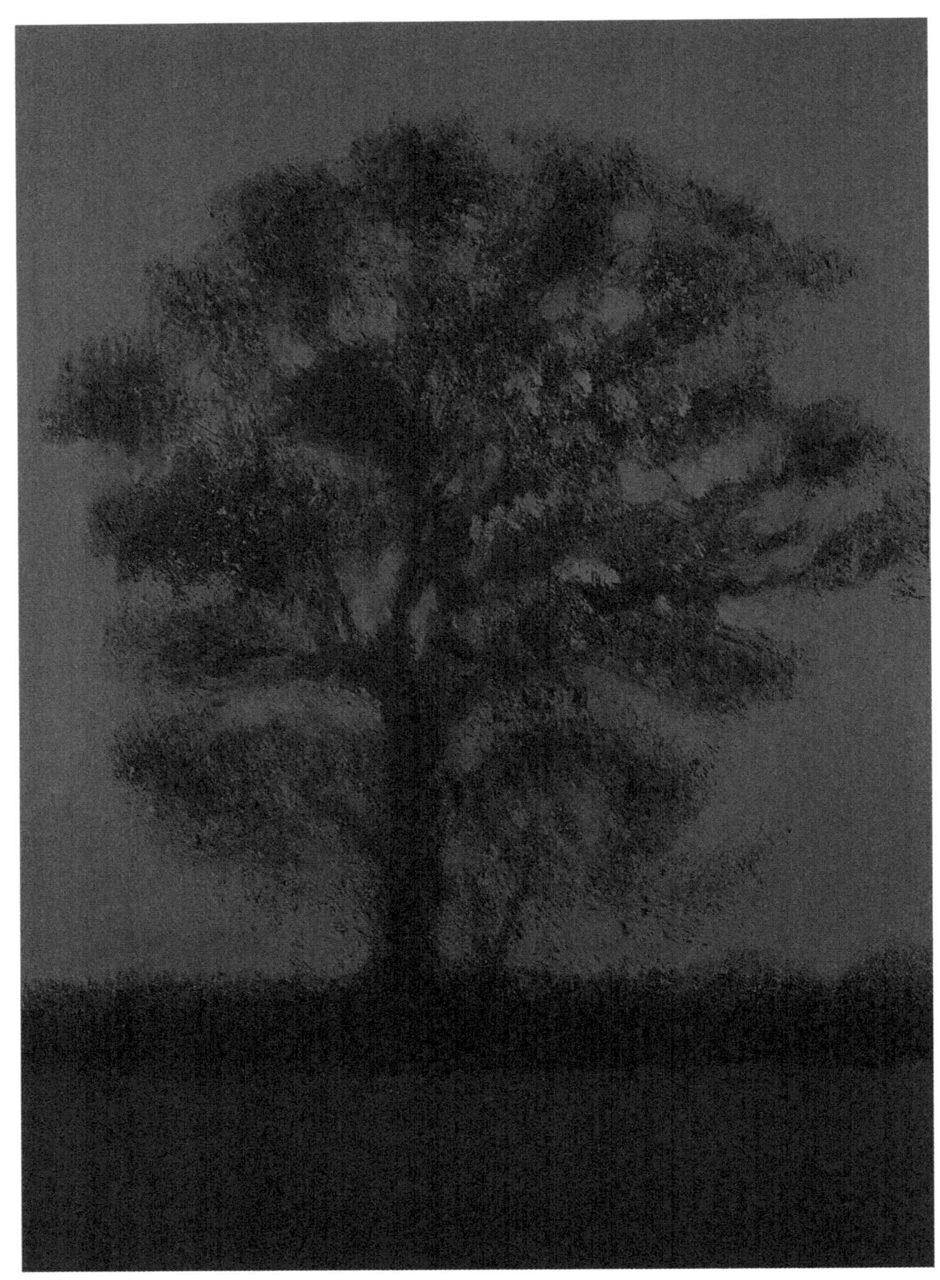

No Moonlight. Oil on board, 183 mm x 130 mm.

It was winter, late at night, and there was no moon. Without moonlight the skyline lacks details, and things are difficult to make out. The shapes at the edges of the field seemed to be at the edge of vision.

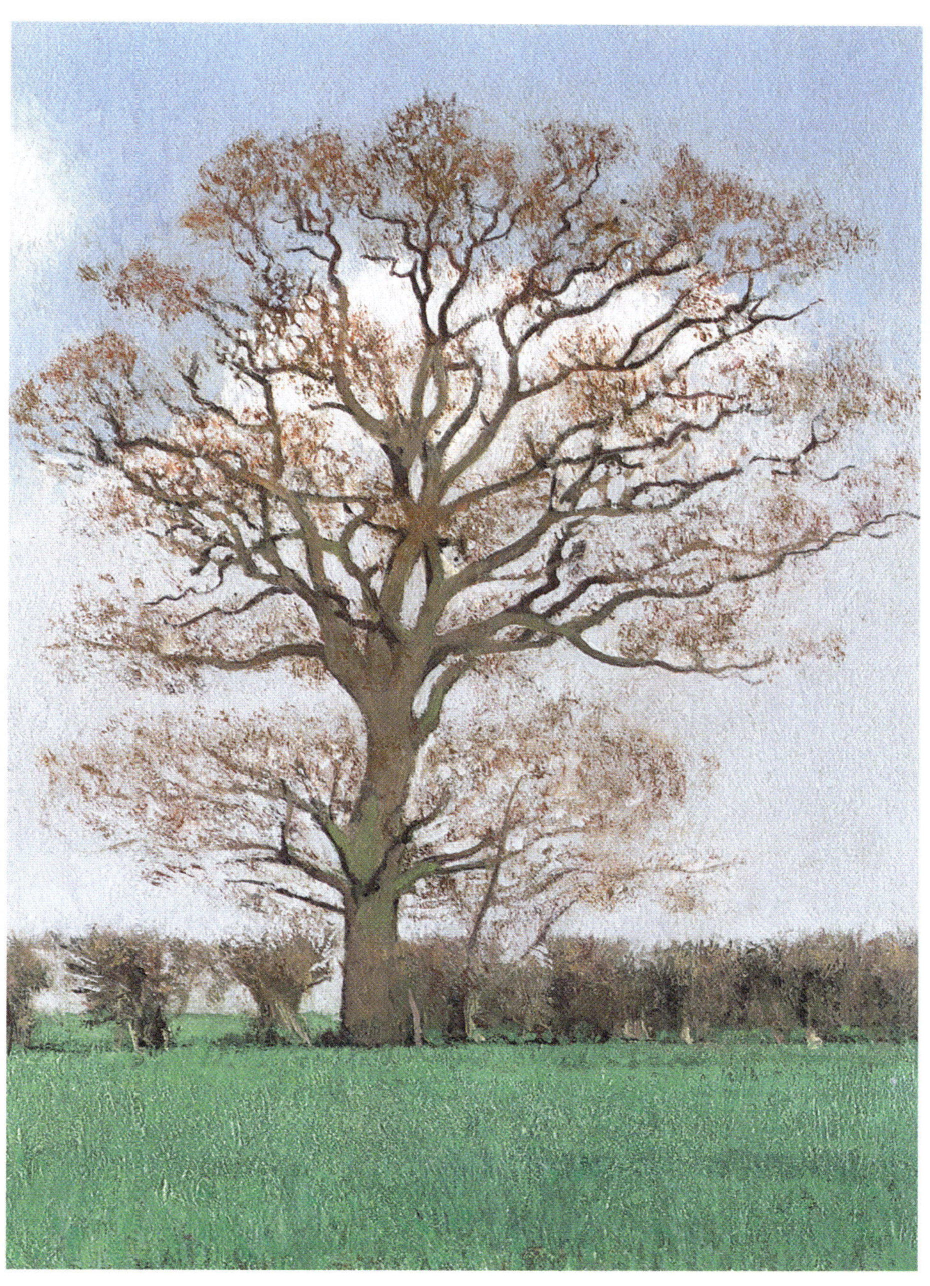

Spring Haze. Oil on board, 183 mm x 130 mm.

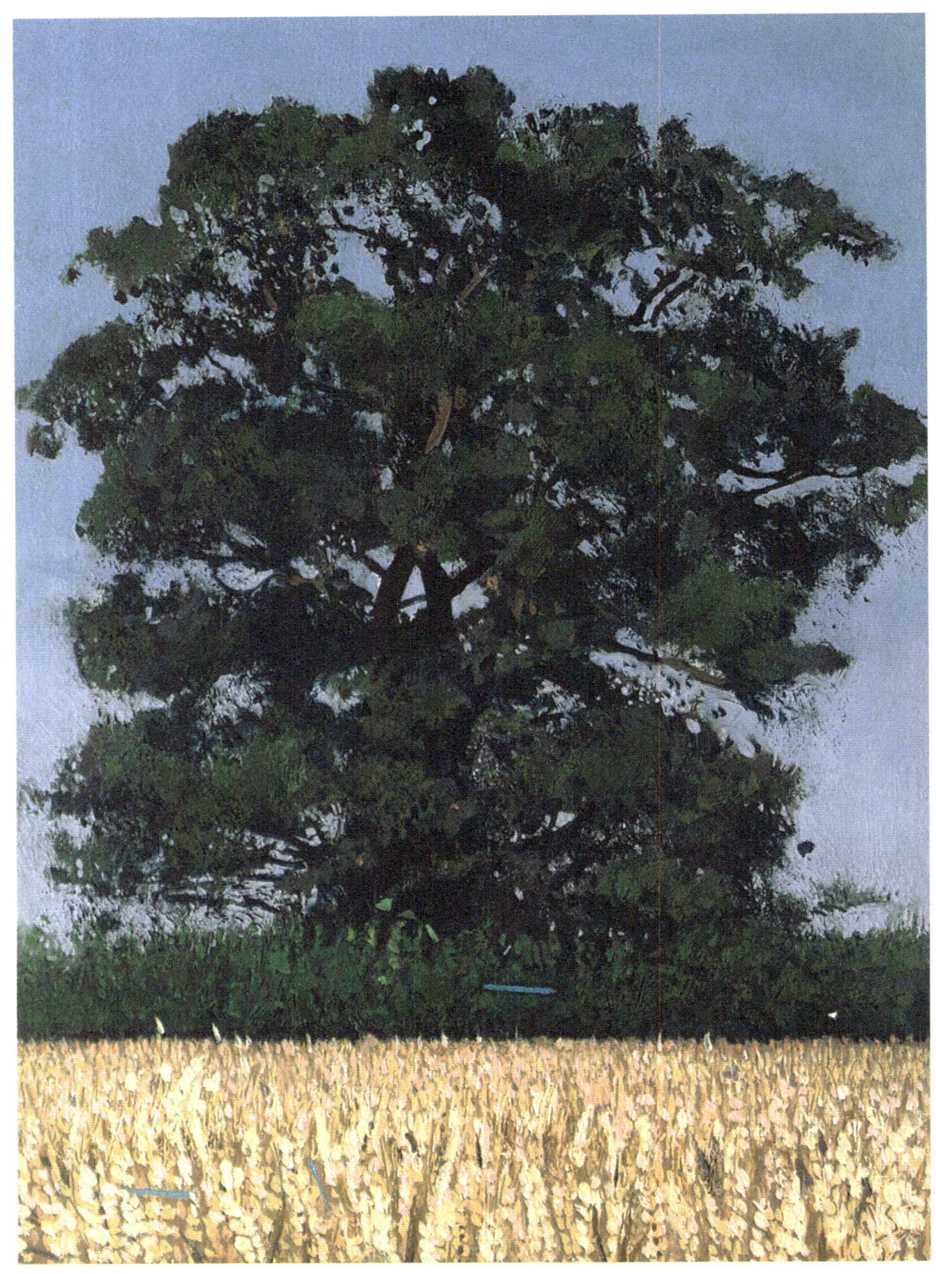

Damsel Flies. Oil on board, 183 mm x 130 mm.

Bill, the farm manager, taught me how to read the harvests. If the wheat grains are dry but the ears have not started to curl over, there can still be a few weeks to go before they are ready to harvest. This indicated how much time I had to finish a painting.

I did hundreds of sessions on the same patch of soil—my own small place. I positioned things in the same way each time: food in the shade of the stool, brushes to the right on a rag so as not to lose them, bags on either side. After I had driven the pole of an umbrella in with a club hammer, I felt as if I'd set camp. I'm easily distracted though: before settling down for this painting, I went back along the wheat tram lines to have another look at a spot of bright red I'd noticed—blood on a dead harvest mouse.

I put on an old T-shirt, sat in the shade of my umbrella, and stared directly at the ensemble of tree, hedge, sky, and crop—nowhere else. The practical problem in these small paintings is how to maximize the definition of each of the four elements—the image is about interrelations, competing and mutually defining colours and textures, not about individual things.

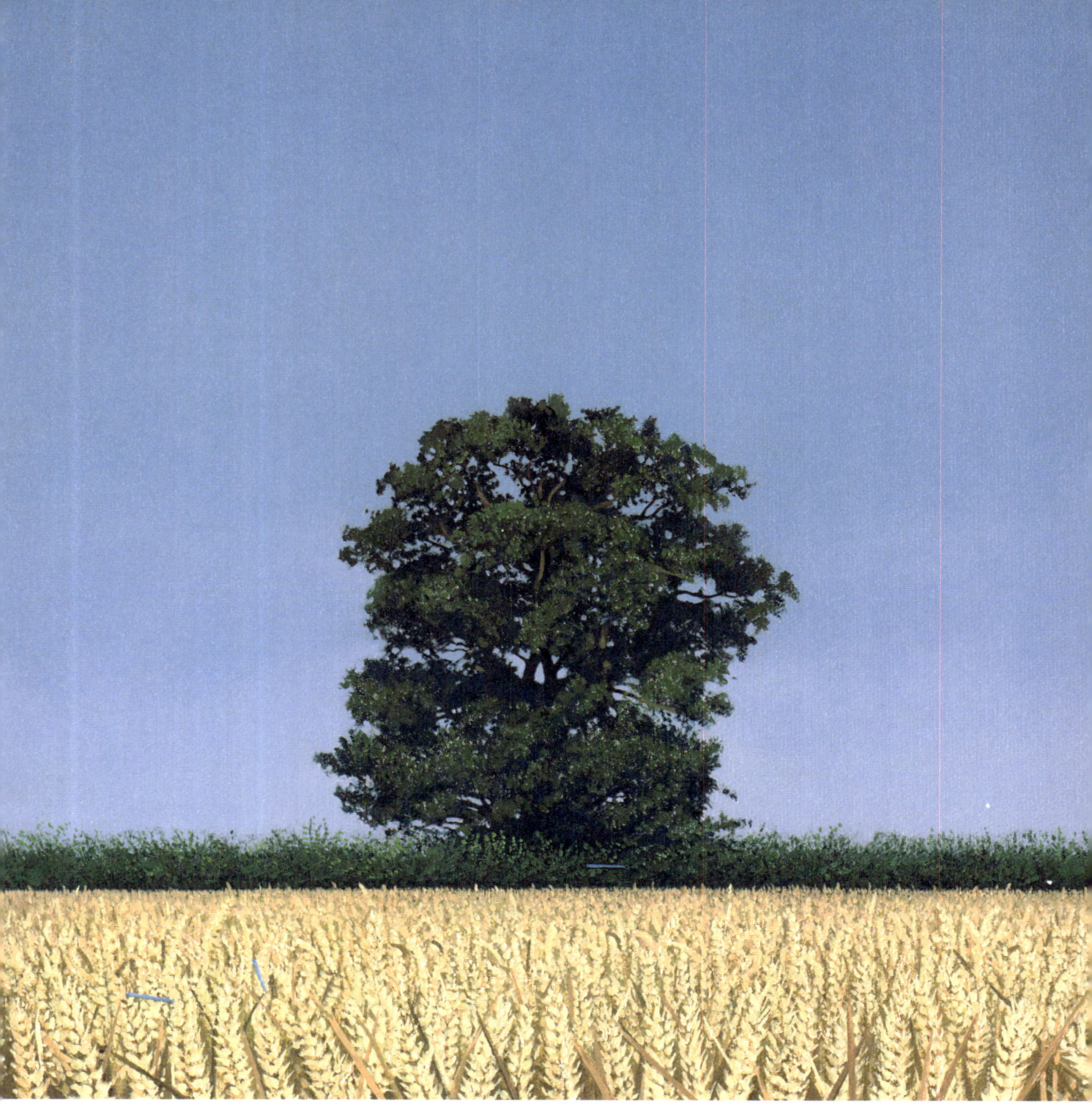

Oak and Wheat. Oil on canvas, 300 mm x 300 mm.

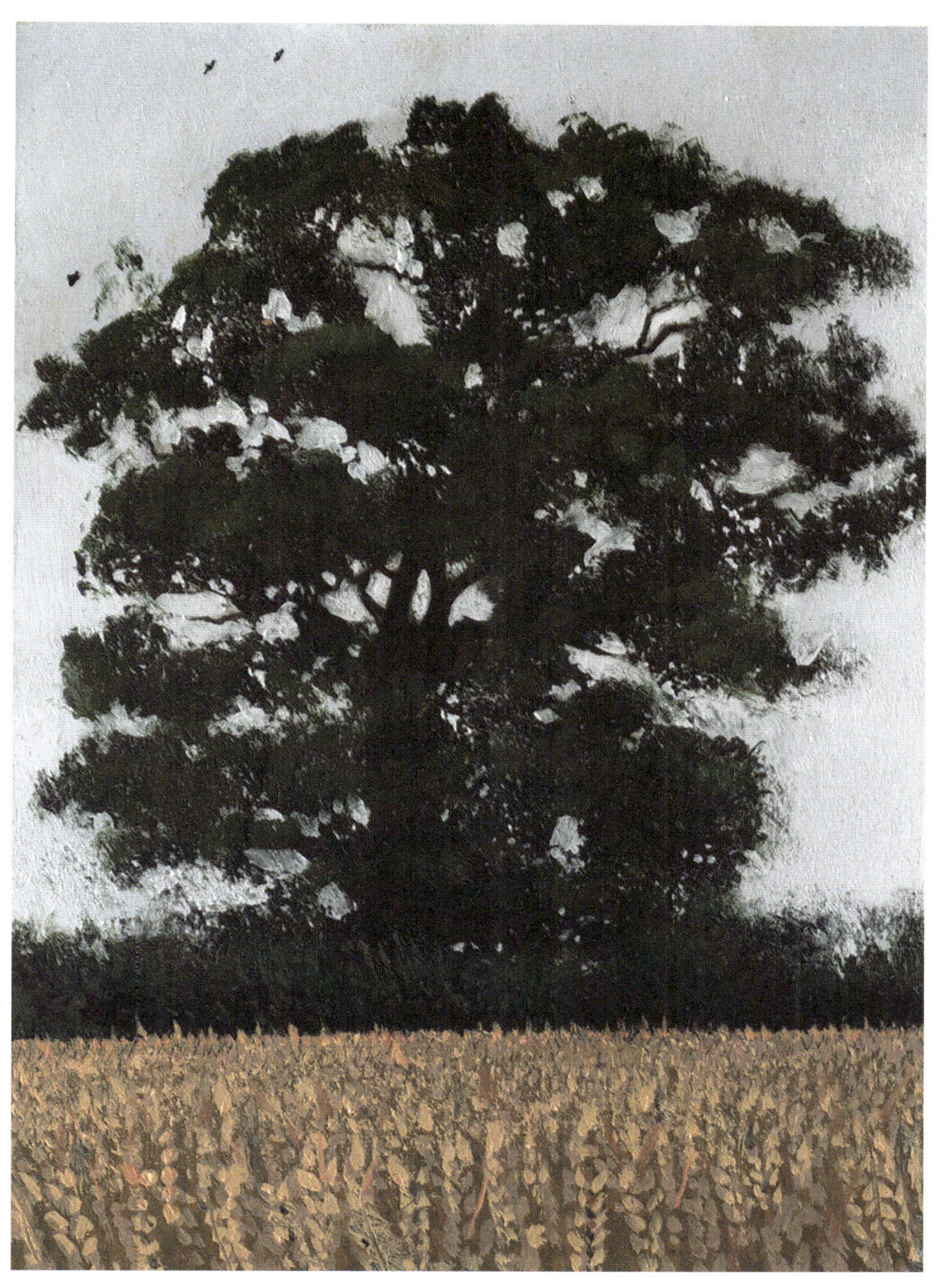

Wheat under Cloud. Oil cn board, 183 mm x 130 mm.

Oak on a Summer Night. Oil on canvas, 300 mm x 300 mm.

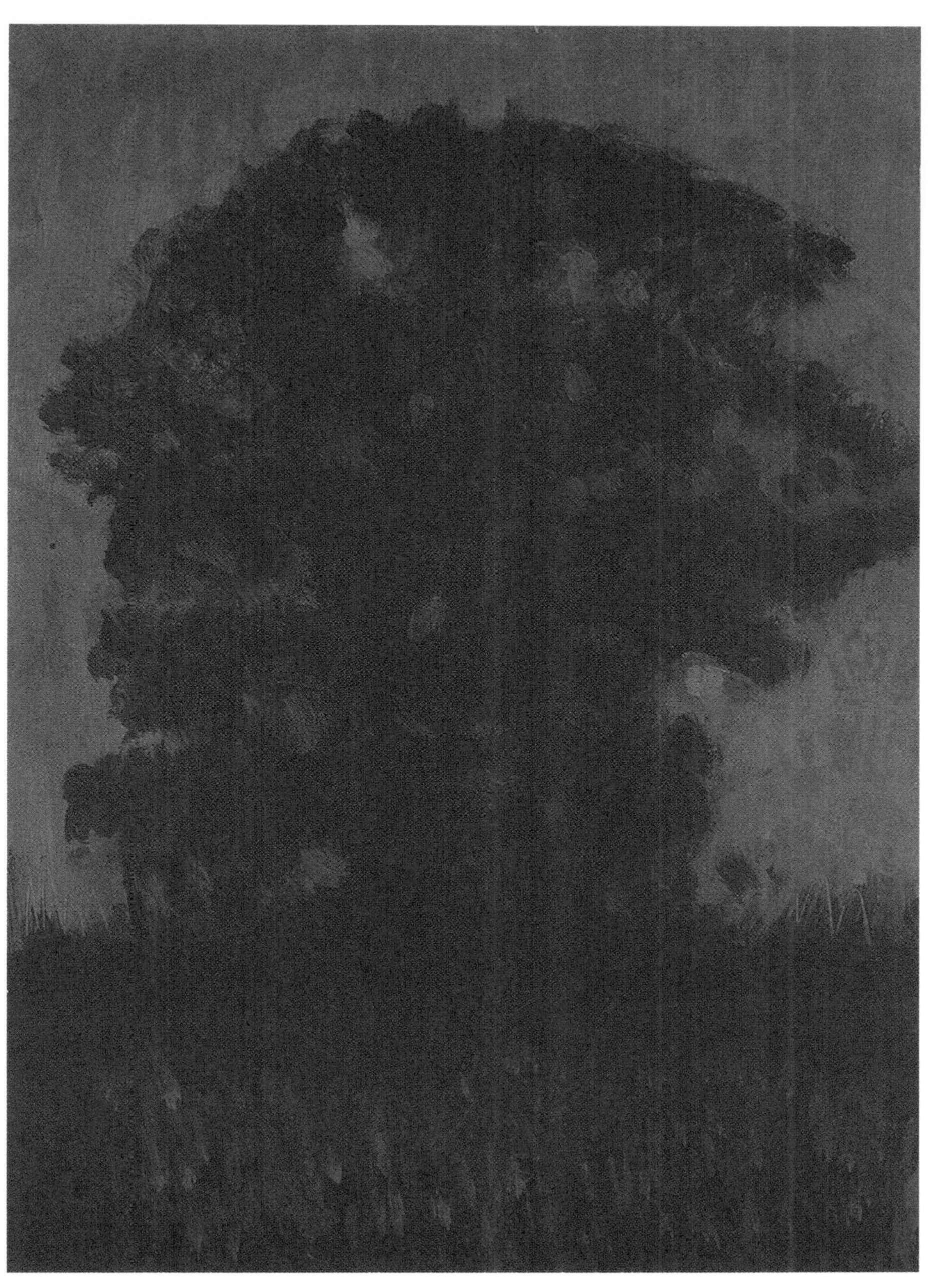

Midsummer Night. Oil on board, 183 mm x 130 mm.

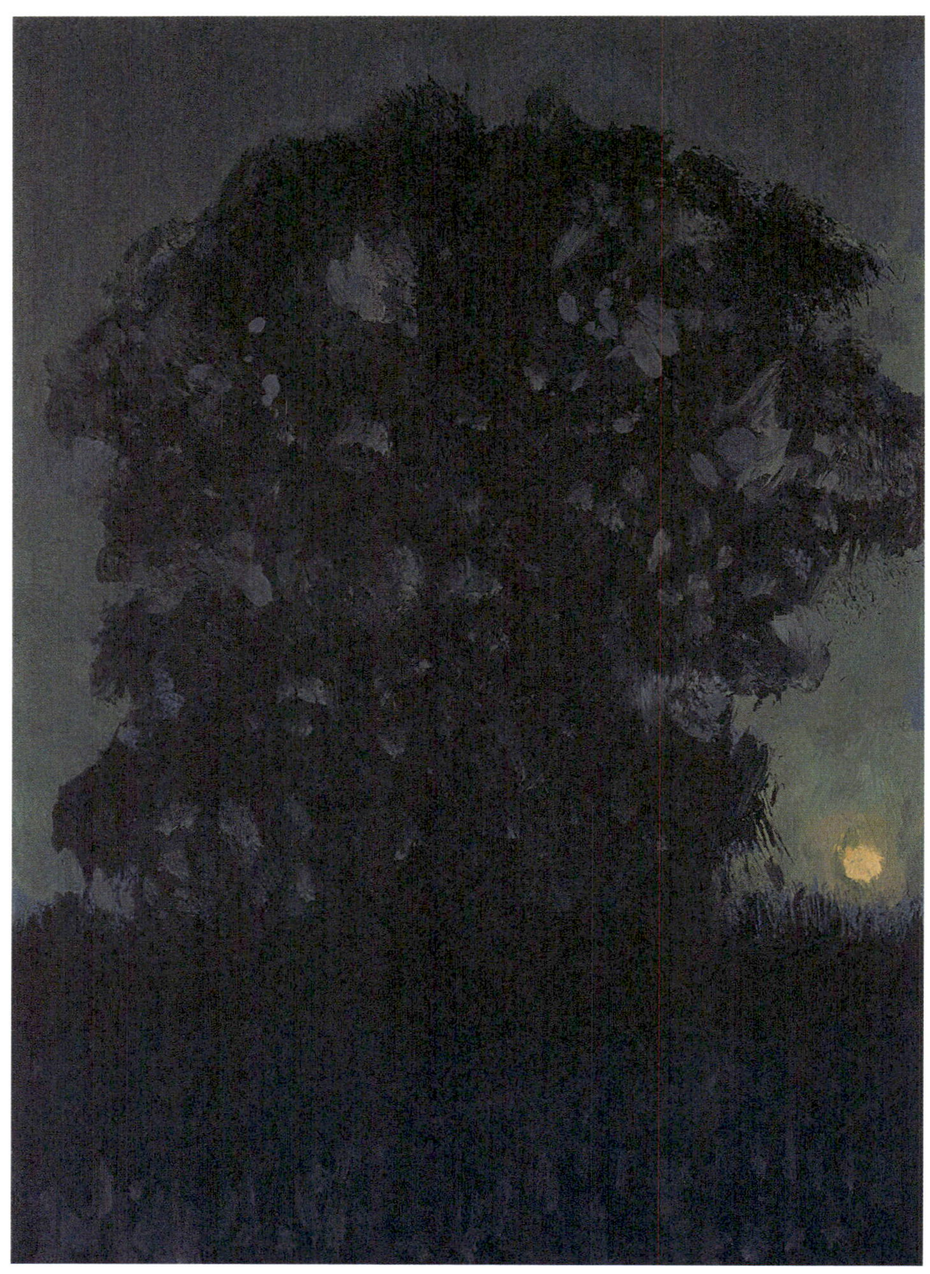

Walking through wheat at night, I was surrounded by what looked like a cora reef spreading into darkness. But I am not lost because I was here a few hours ago, painting under a blue sky.

There is so much green in the early night sky, it reminds me of an aquarium. At night different objects emerge: a distant house light, a star, and the dome of my umbrella, now like a black mushroom. I switch on a small torch strung round my neck. Its light is so weak that it barely affects my eyes, already adjusted to the dark. Looking down I now see familiar things: paints, bags, camping seat.

Settling in, I put a fresh board inside the open lid of the painting box on my lap. The moon is just within my field of vision. The oak now has sharp, black, lacy edges with little holes of sky inside. The sky changes to yellow-green closer to the moon and fades to darker and redder colour away from it. The tree sits between these two colour fields with the blackest shade in the centre at its base where I can see nothing. Nothing at all. The painting could be built on this: a tree and faint wheat heads floating round blackness, emerging into colour and shape.

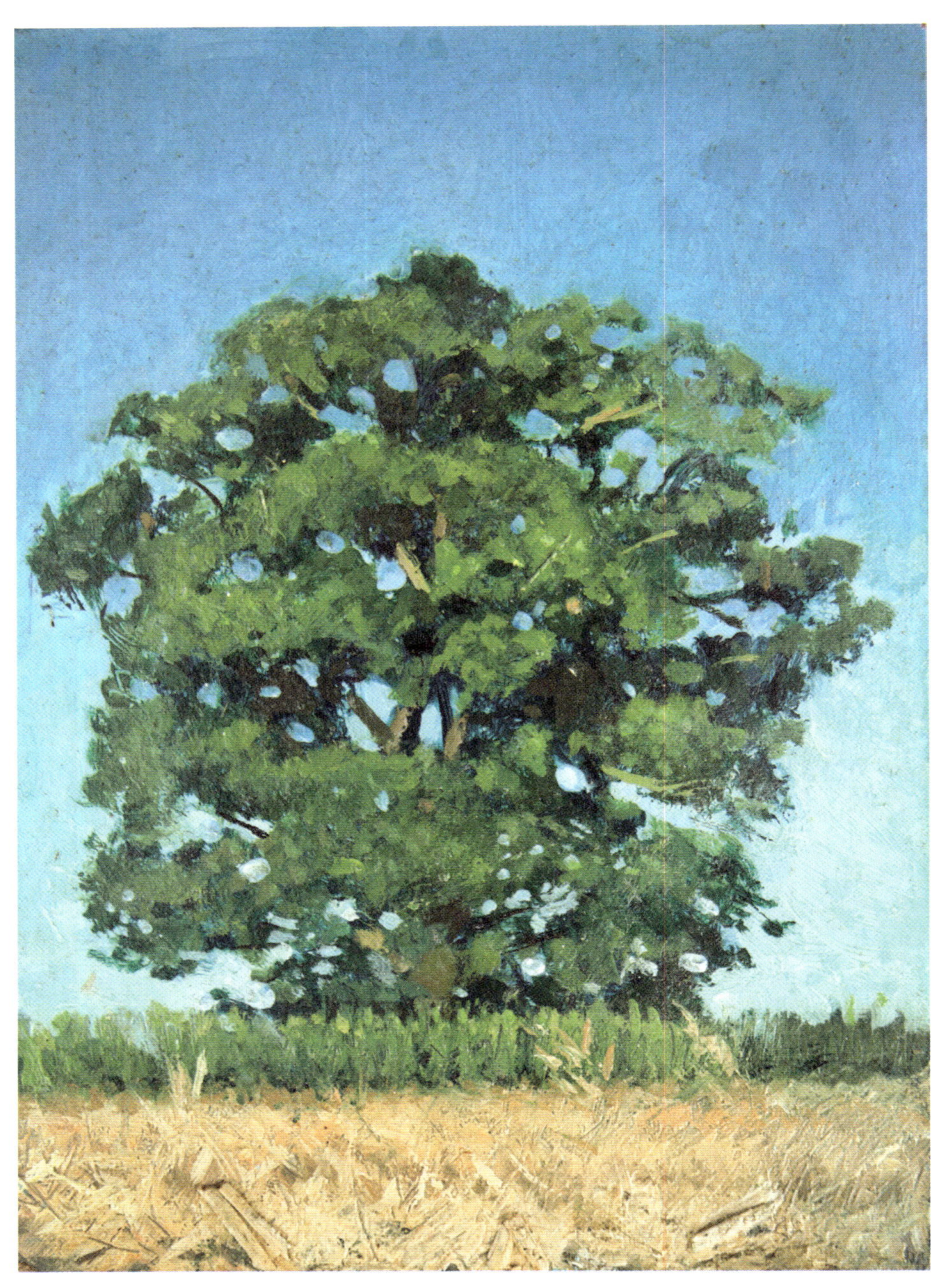

Oak with Real Wheat Stalks. Oil on board, 160 mm x 115 mm.

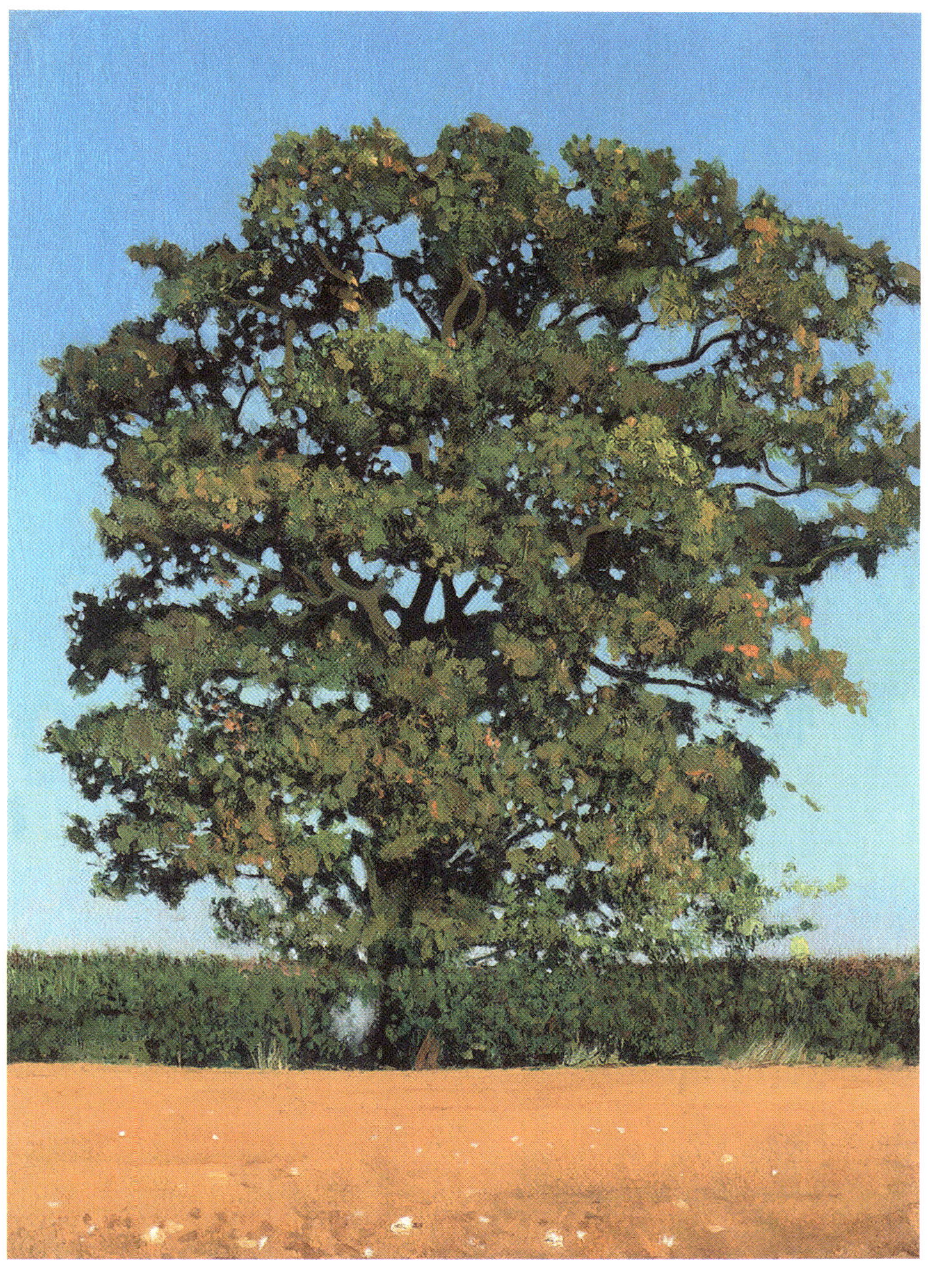

Cut Hedge. Oil on board, 183 mm x 130 mm.

The hazel hedge has just been cut and the field prepared for sowing winter barley, the next crop in the field rotation. Barley is able to survive in poor conditions and so is sown after a nutrient-hungry crop like wheat.

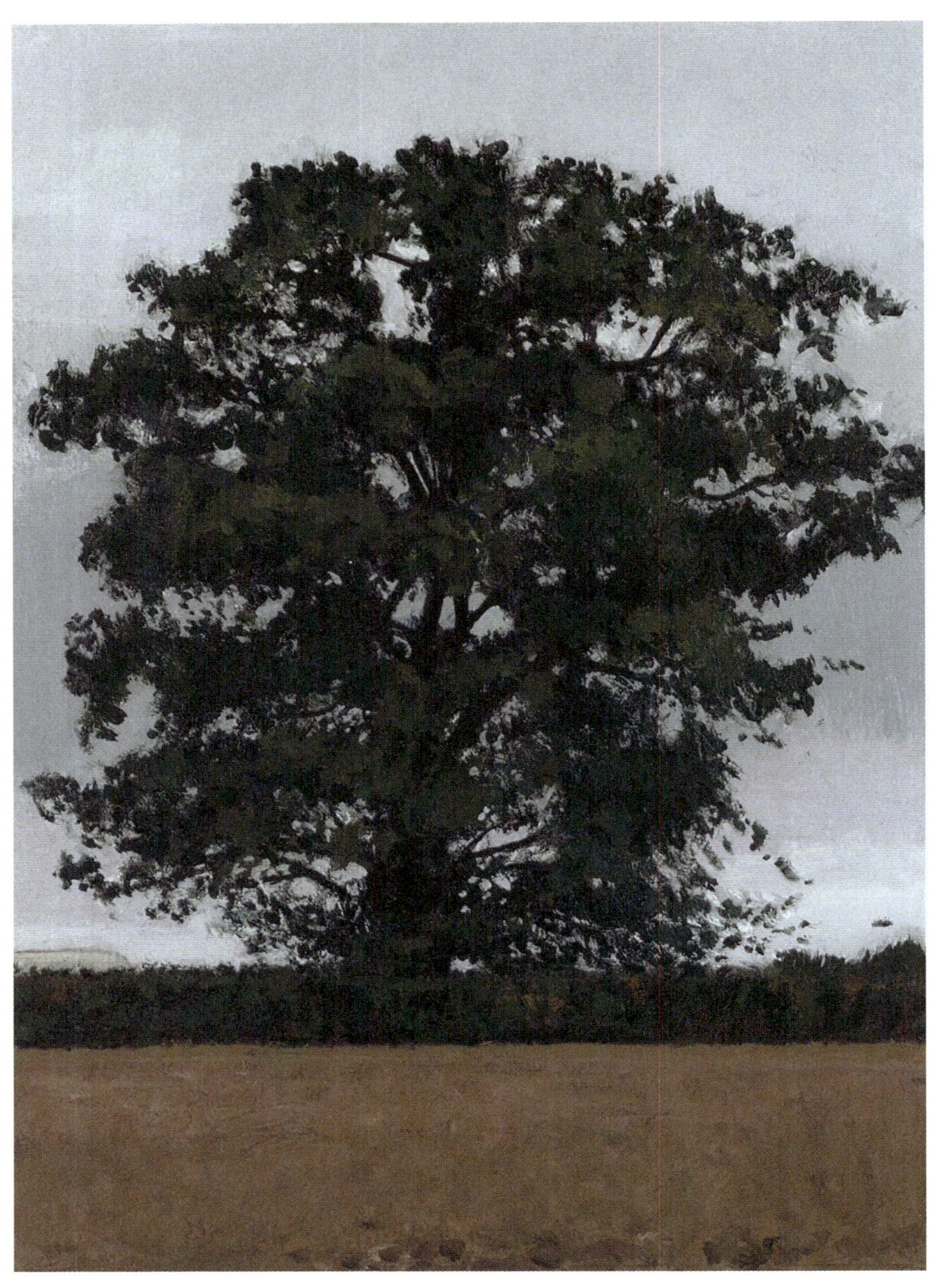

Caravan. Oil on board, 183 mm x 130 mm.

Opposite: *Flock of Pigeons.* Oil on canvas, 910 mm x 660 mm.

Overleaf: *Flock of Pigeons,* detail

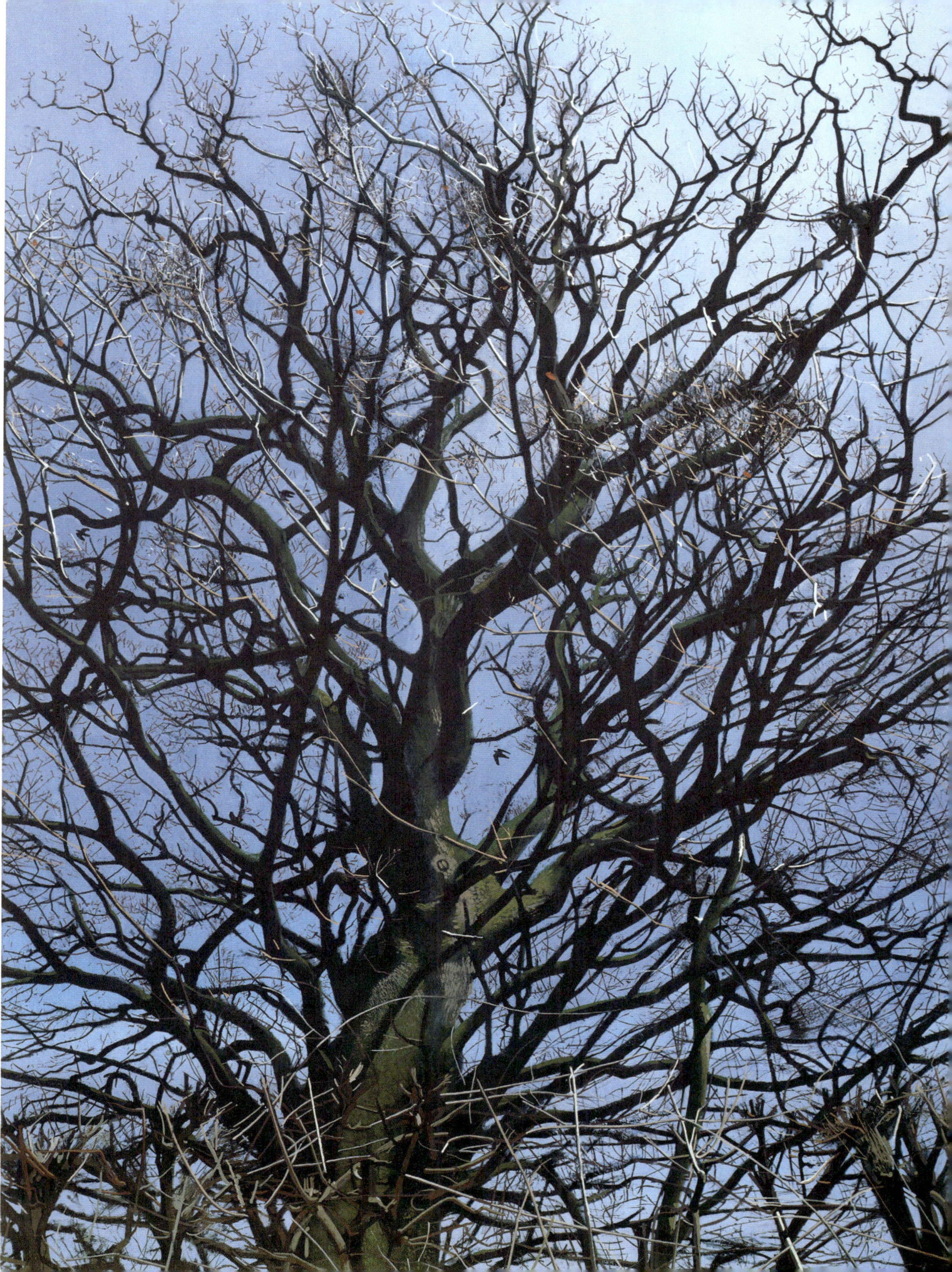

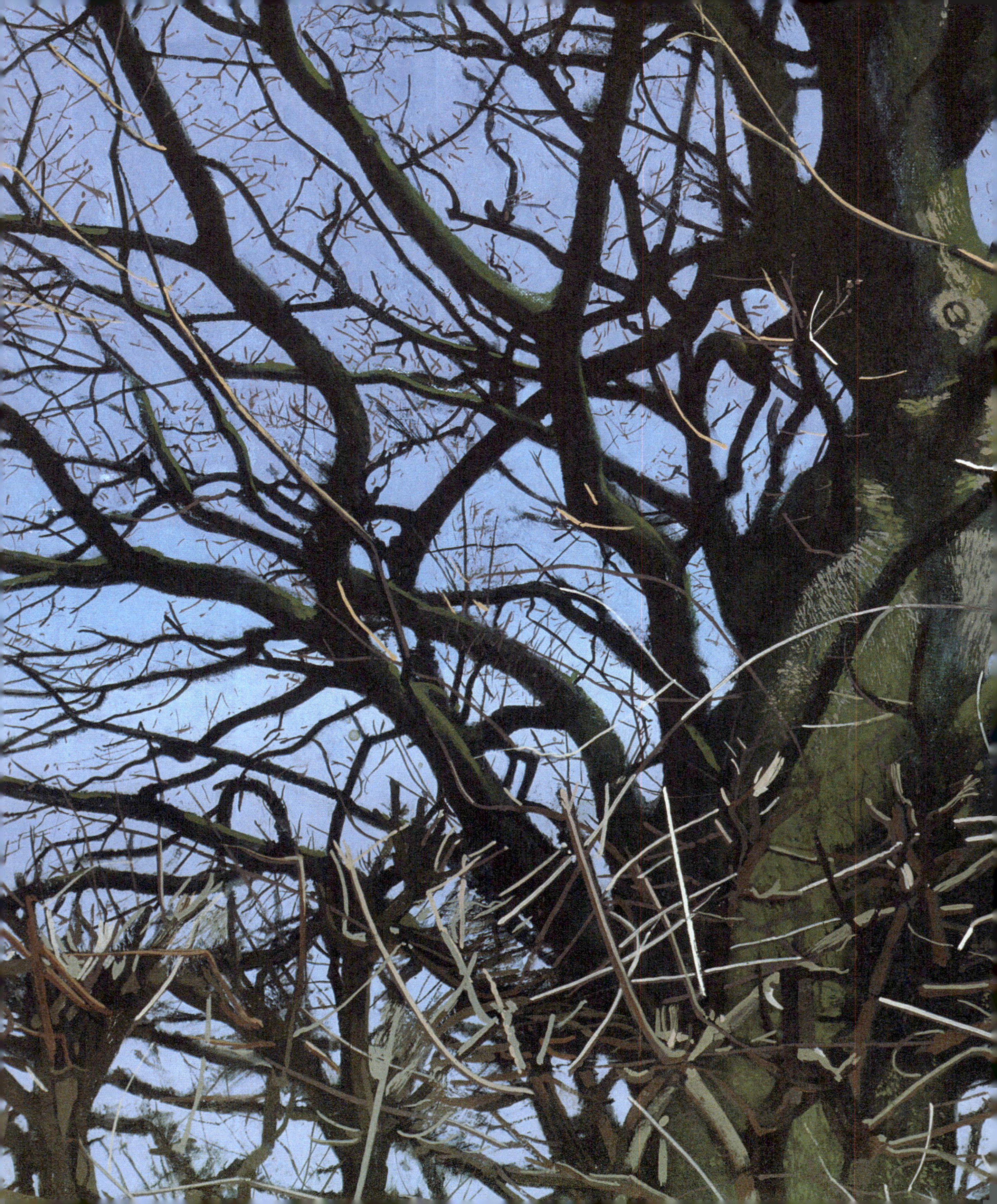

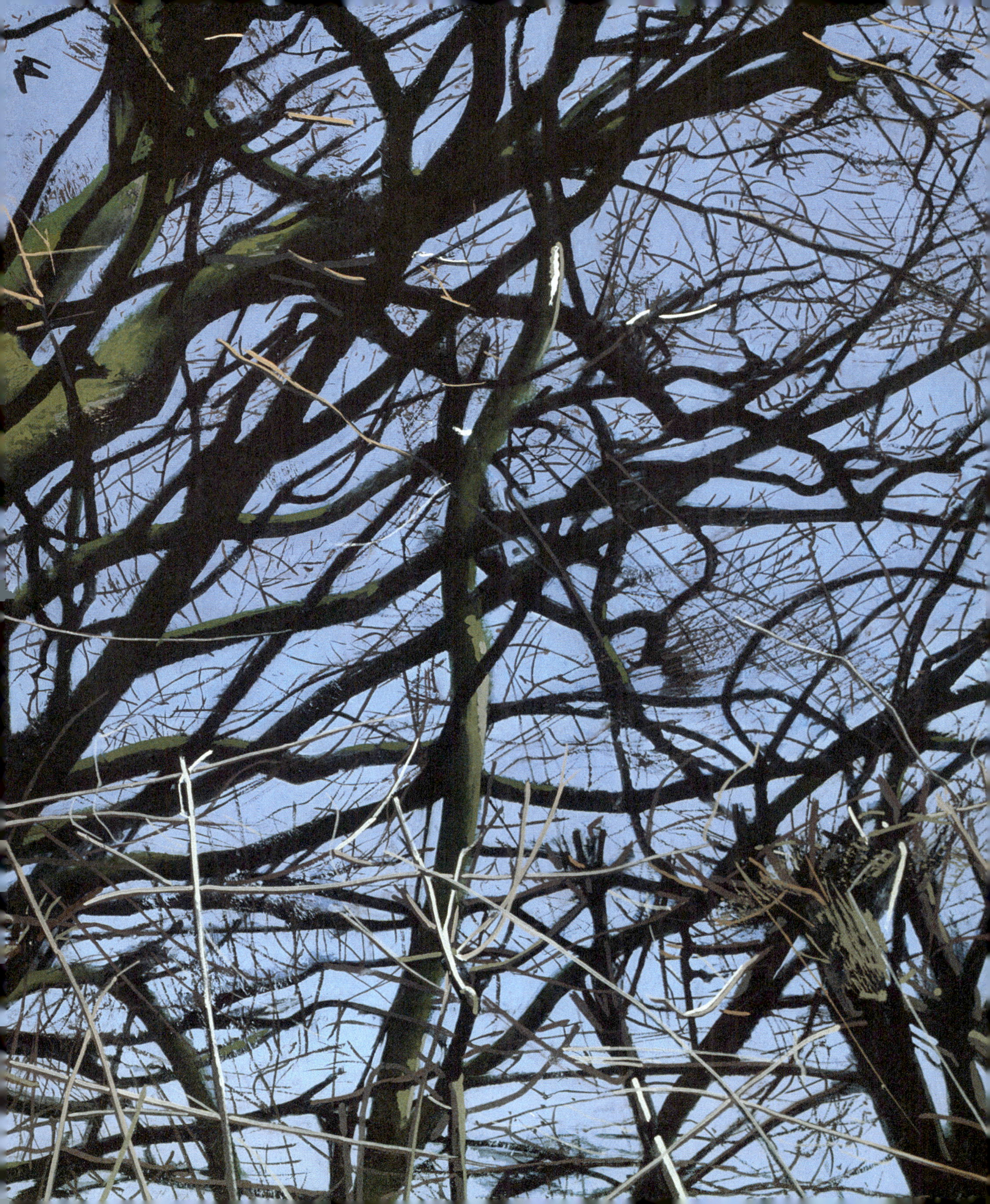

Lunar Eclipse and Orion, West Bergholt. Oil on canvas, 1220 mm x 910 mm.
The oak on the east side of the field also showed up well at night. Here it is
under a lunar eclipse.
Opposite: *Oak at Night.* Oil on canvas, 920 mm x 660 mm.

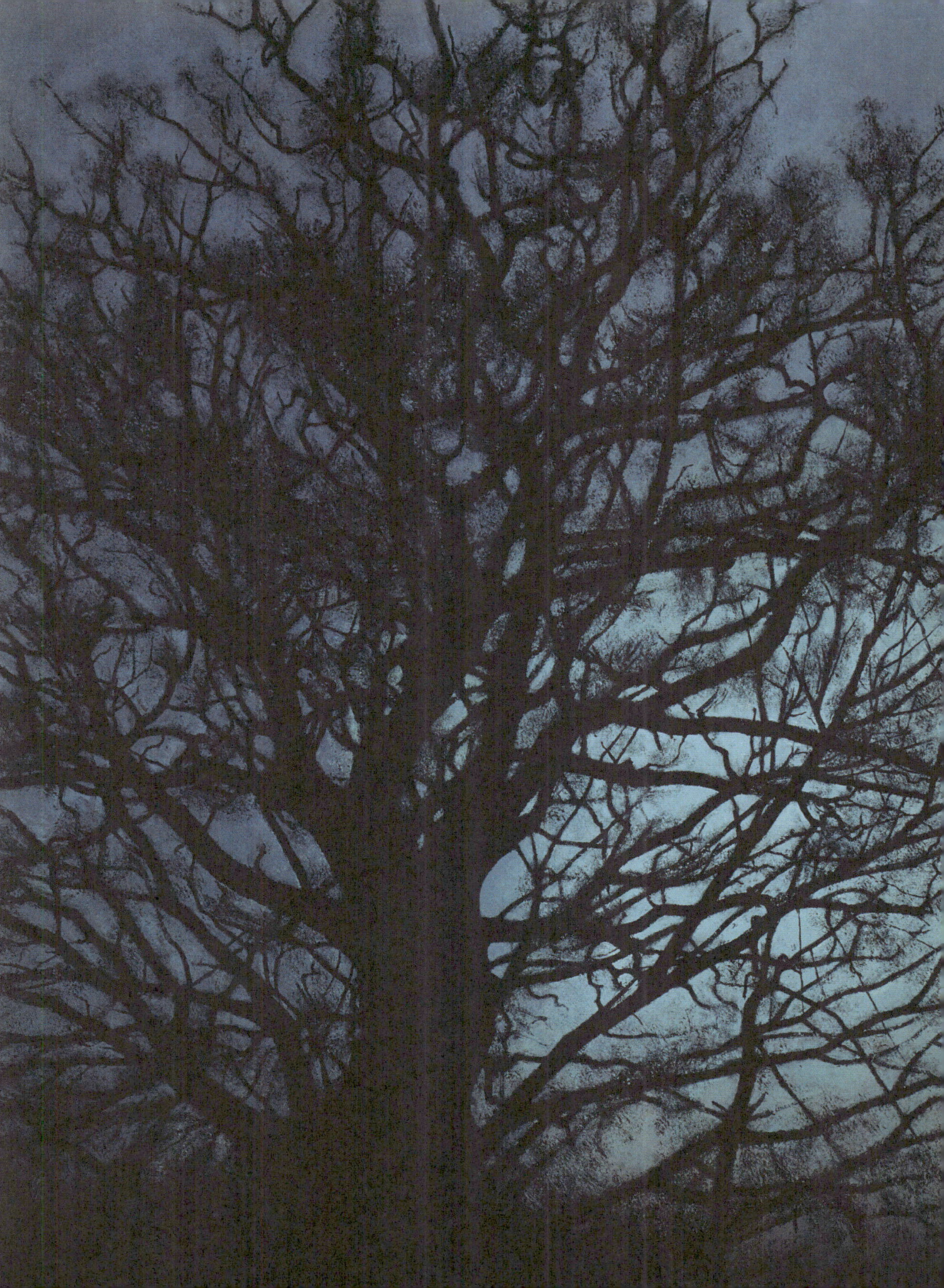

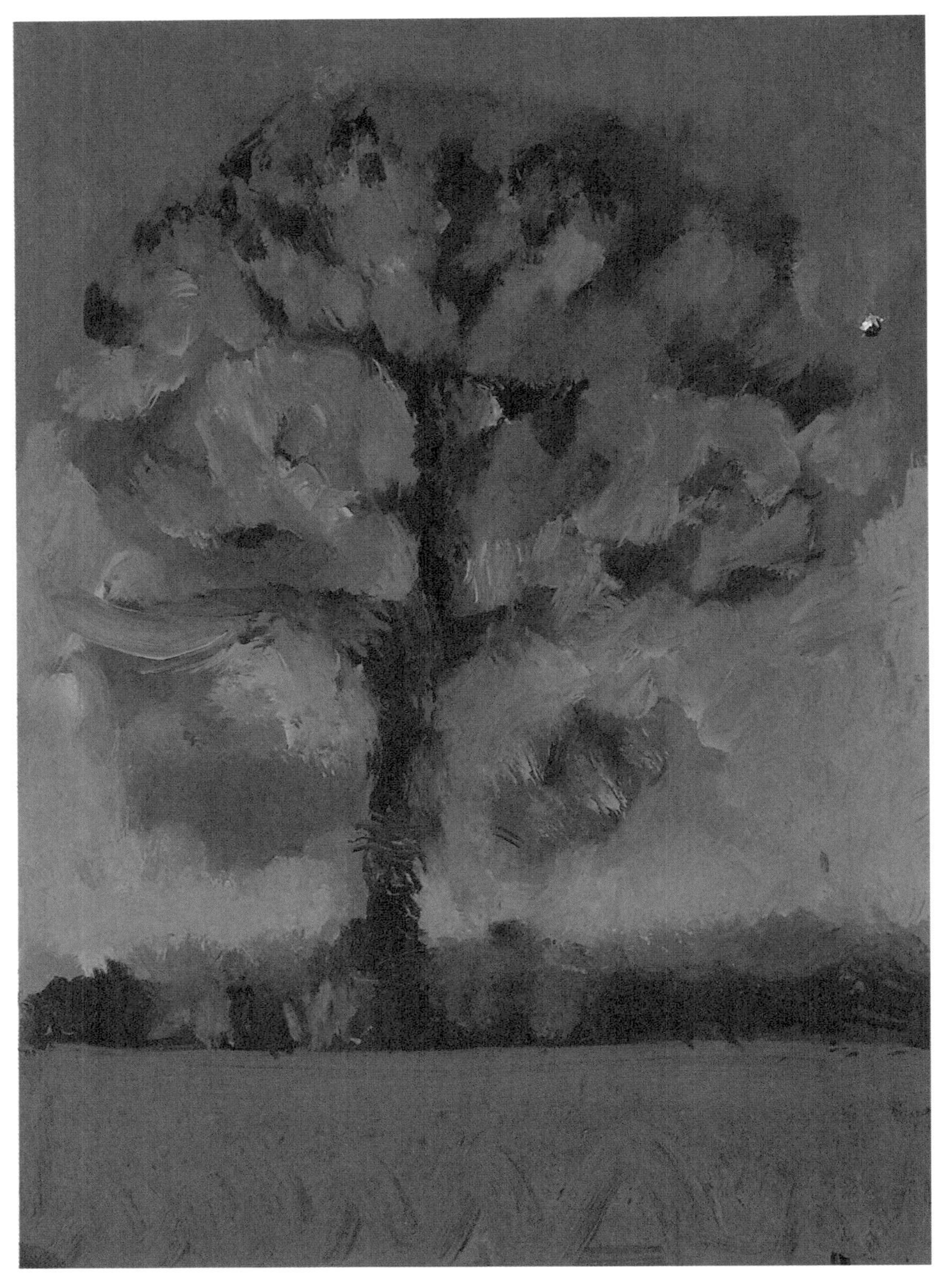

Tree Painted without Artificial Light. Oil on board, 183 mm x 130 mm.
What would a painting of an oak tree look like made at night with no
moonlight and no artificial illumination?

Painting is an art that brings things in and out of visibility, and
nighttime can be of special interest to artists. Painting at night usually
involves artificial light to brighten the work surface to about the level
present in the landscape. No such light was used here, and only very
low ambient light reflected off of the board. In low light the resolution
power of the eye falls, and only very broad colour areas are visible to
the painter—hence the big brush marks. The bright yellow spot was a
plane on its way to London Stansted.

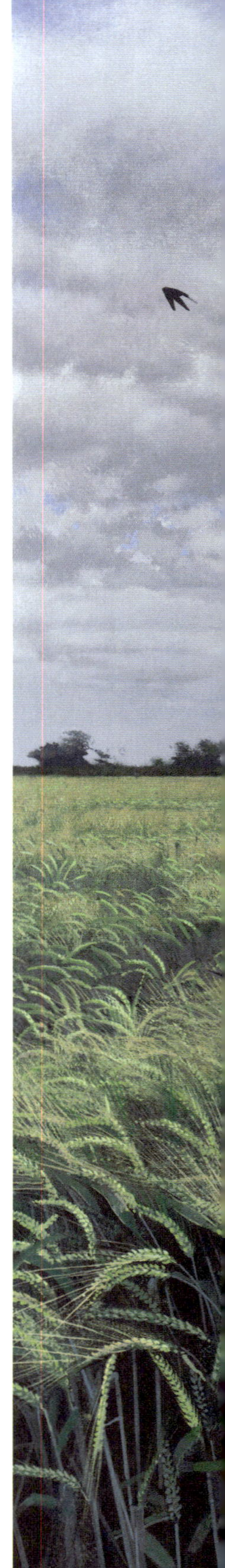

Swallows at 11am, first version. Oil on canvas, 1020 mm x 1020 mm.
When I was painting this, at the back of my mind was "Burnt Norton," a poem from *Four Quartets* (1944) by T. S. Eliot that associates a tree with "the still point of the turning world." (For studies of this painting, see page 112.)

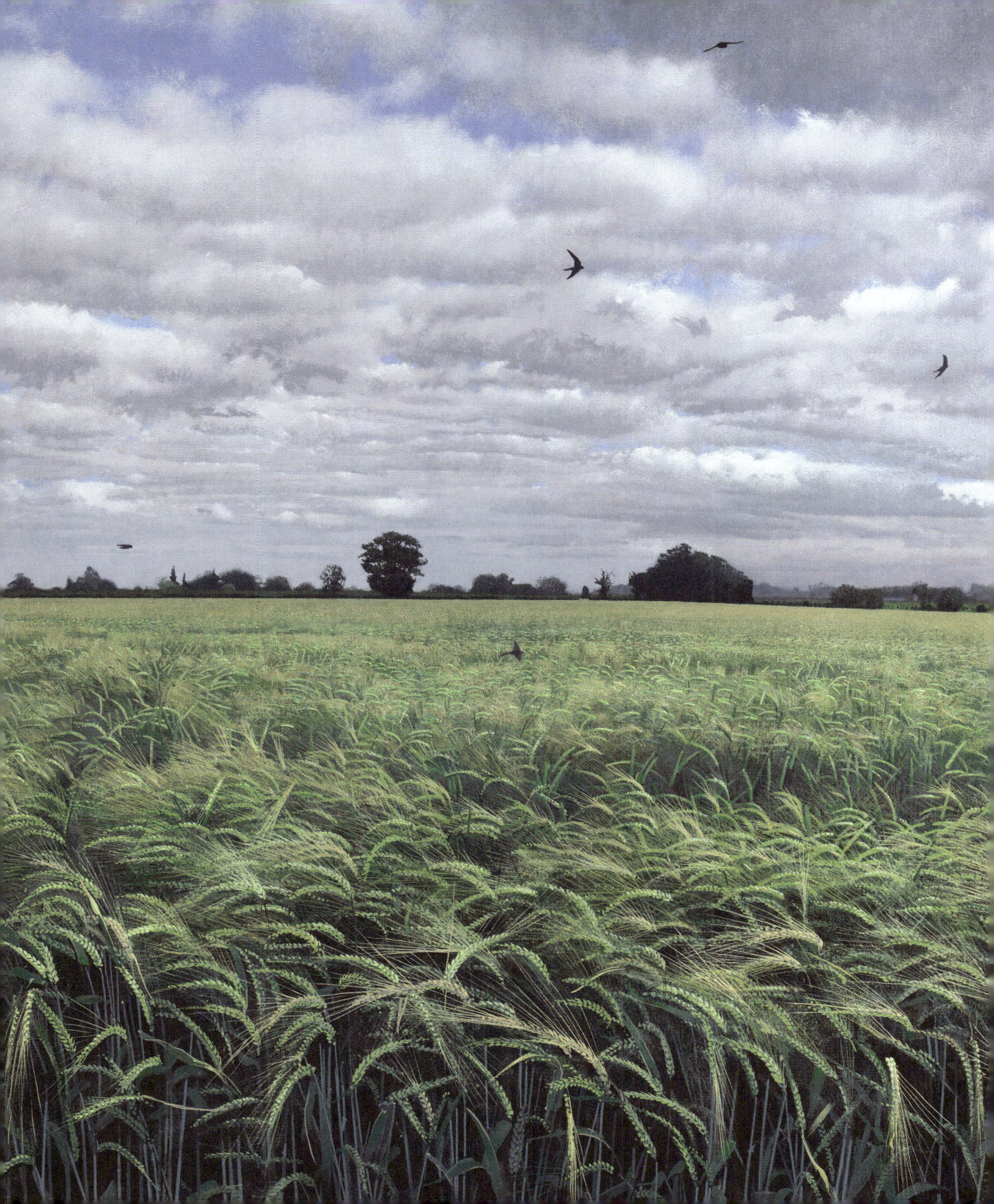

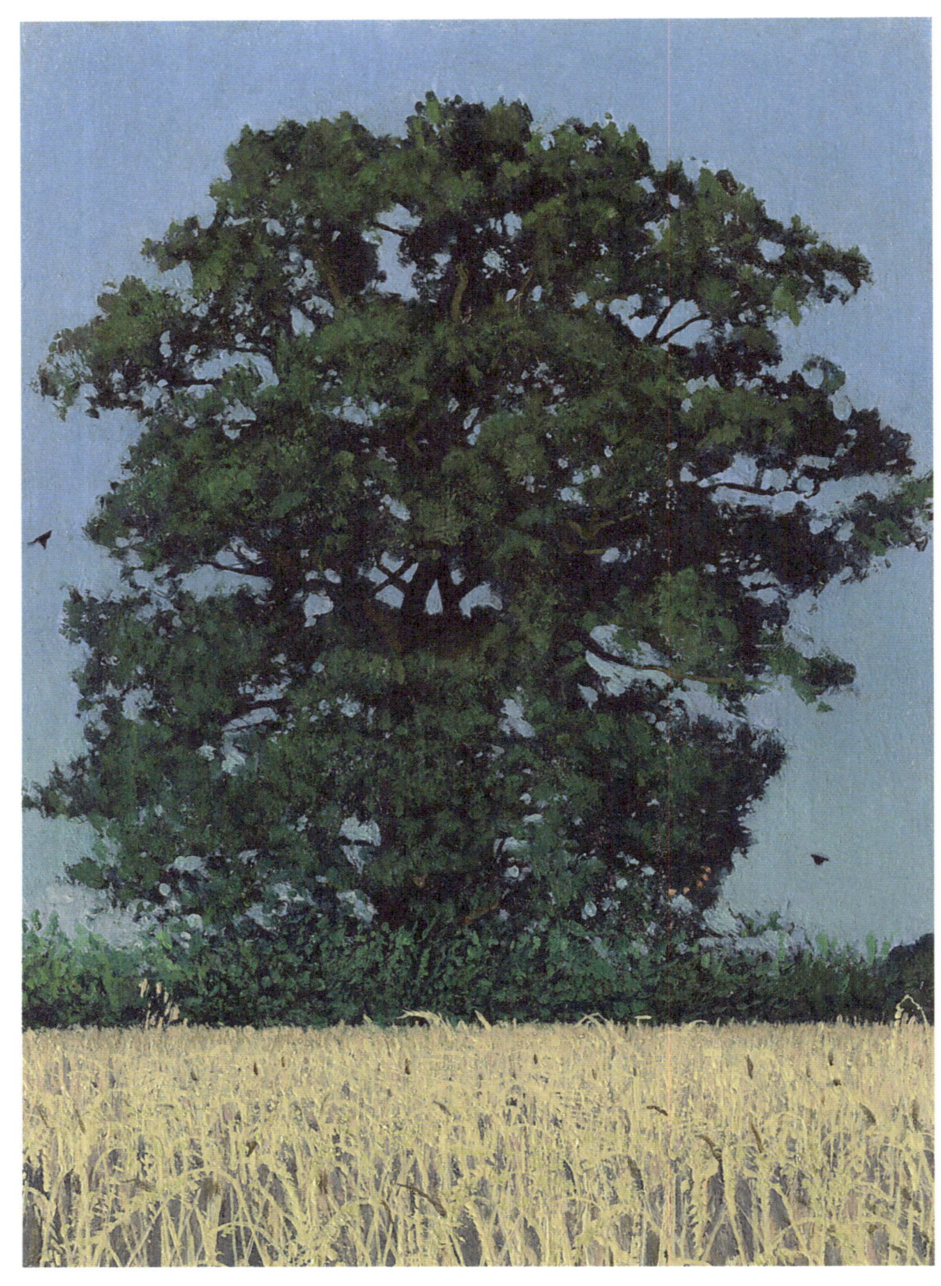

Blackbirds. Oil on board, 183 mm x 130 mm.

Opposite: *Blue Tit Foraging on Pollard Branch.* Oil on canvas, 910 mm x 660 mm.

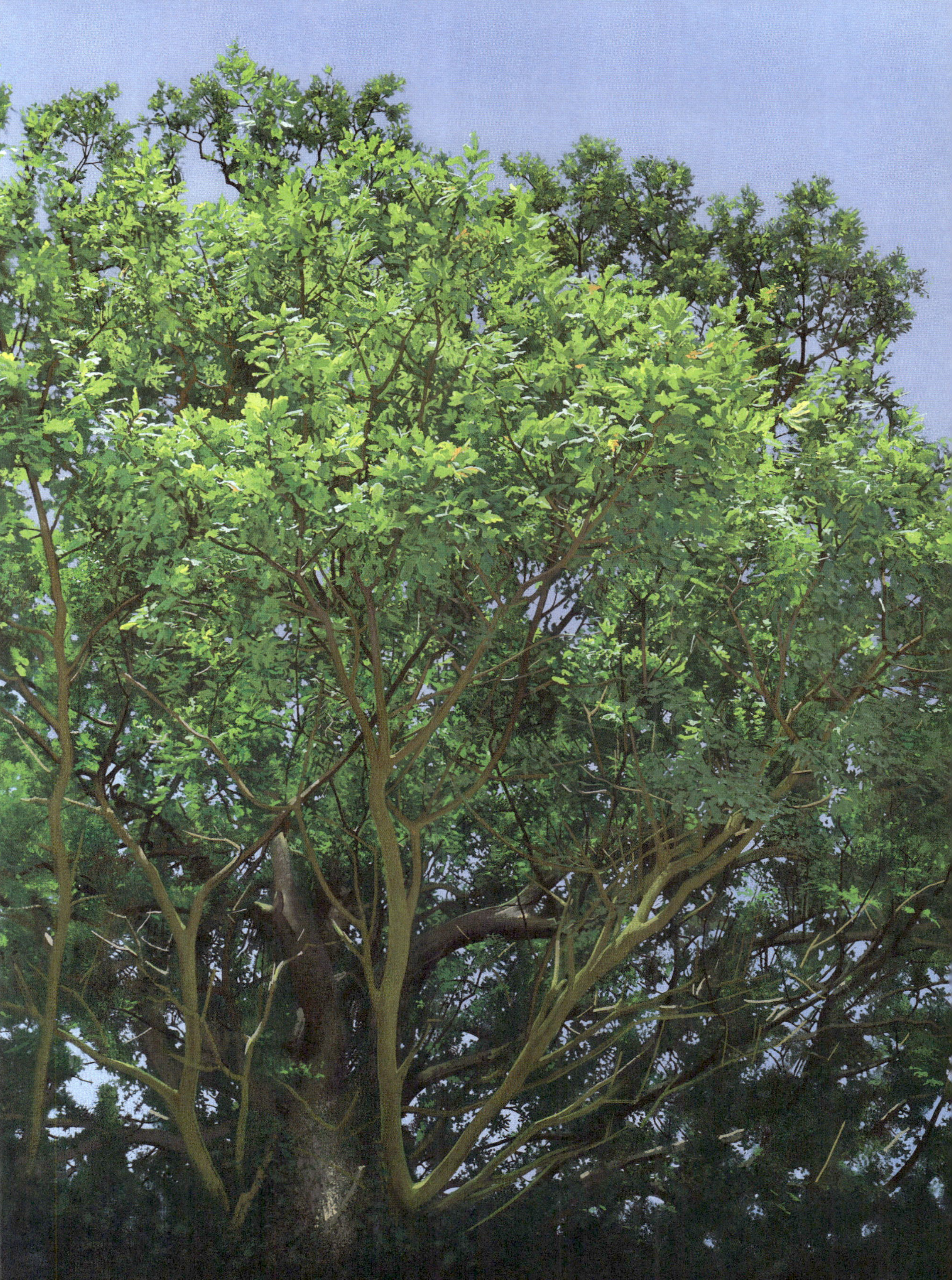

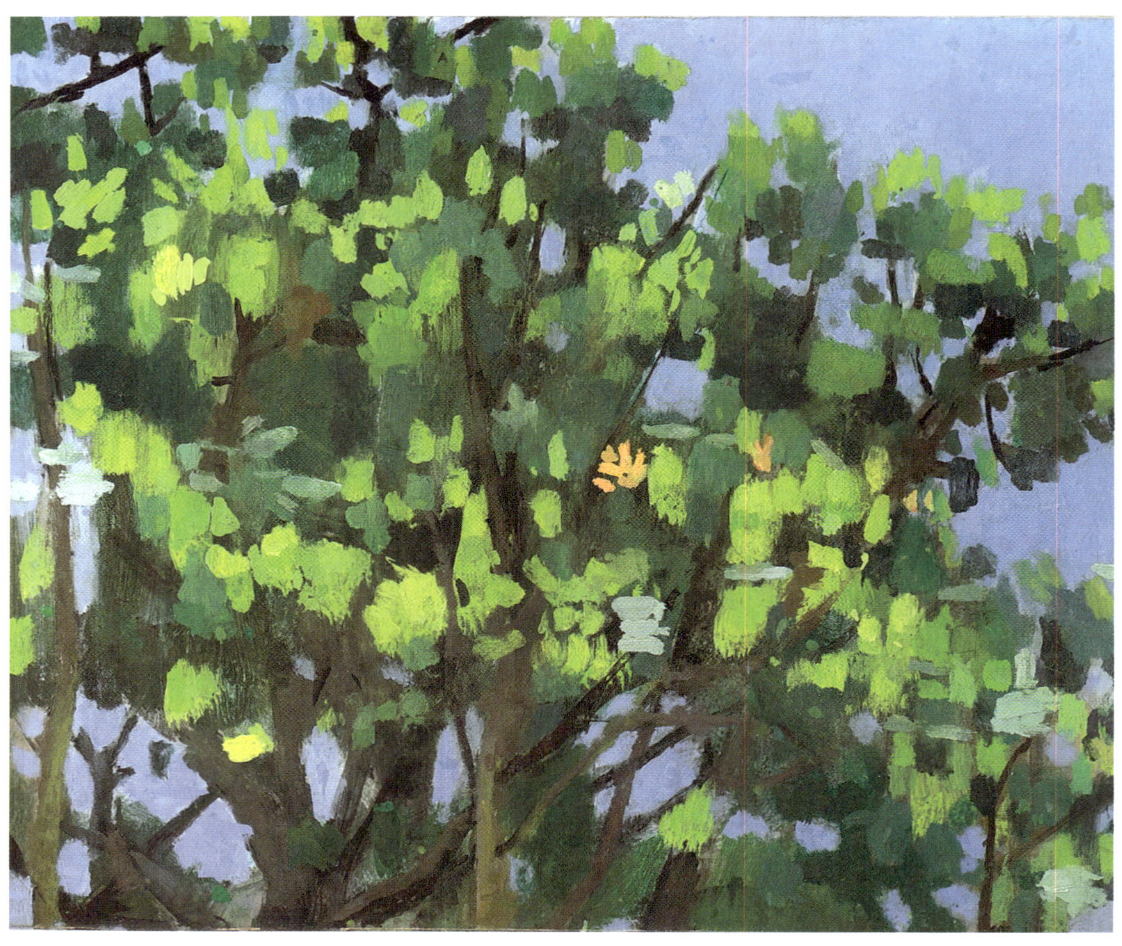

Two finished studies for *Blue Tit Foraging on Pollard Branch*. Oil on board, 360 mm x 300 mm.
The approach here was Cezanne inspired. I painted these without glasses
(I'm nearsighted) to help me to attend to the colours—one colour world of the
leaves of the outer canopy and another within the lower branches.

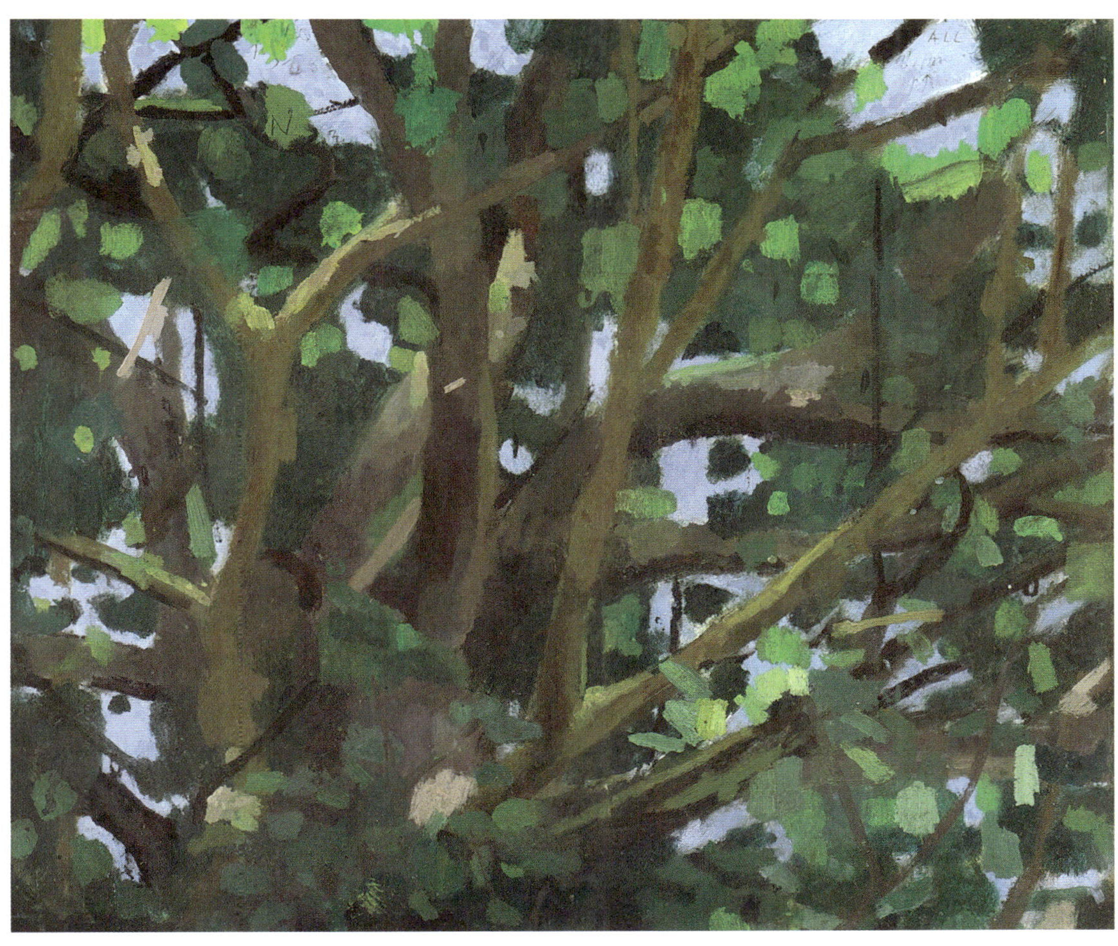

Blue Tit Foraging on Pollard Branch, detail.
The paler branches are pollard branches. Oak branches have a zigzag growth
pattern that evolved to fit leaves into light-catching spaces in canopies of
competing trees. But if an oak loses a low branch, it conserves energy by
shooting out a pollard branch—leaves appear only at the tips, where the
sunlight is.

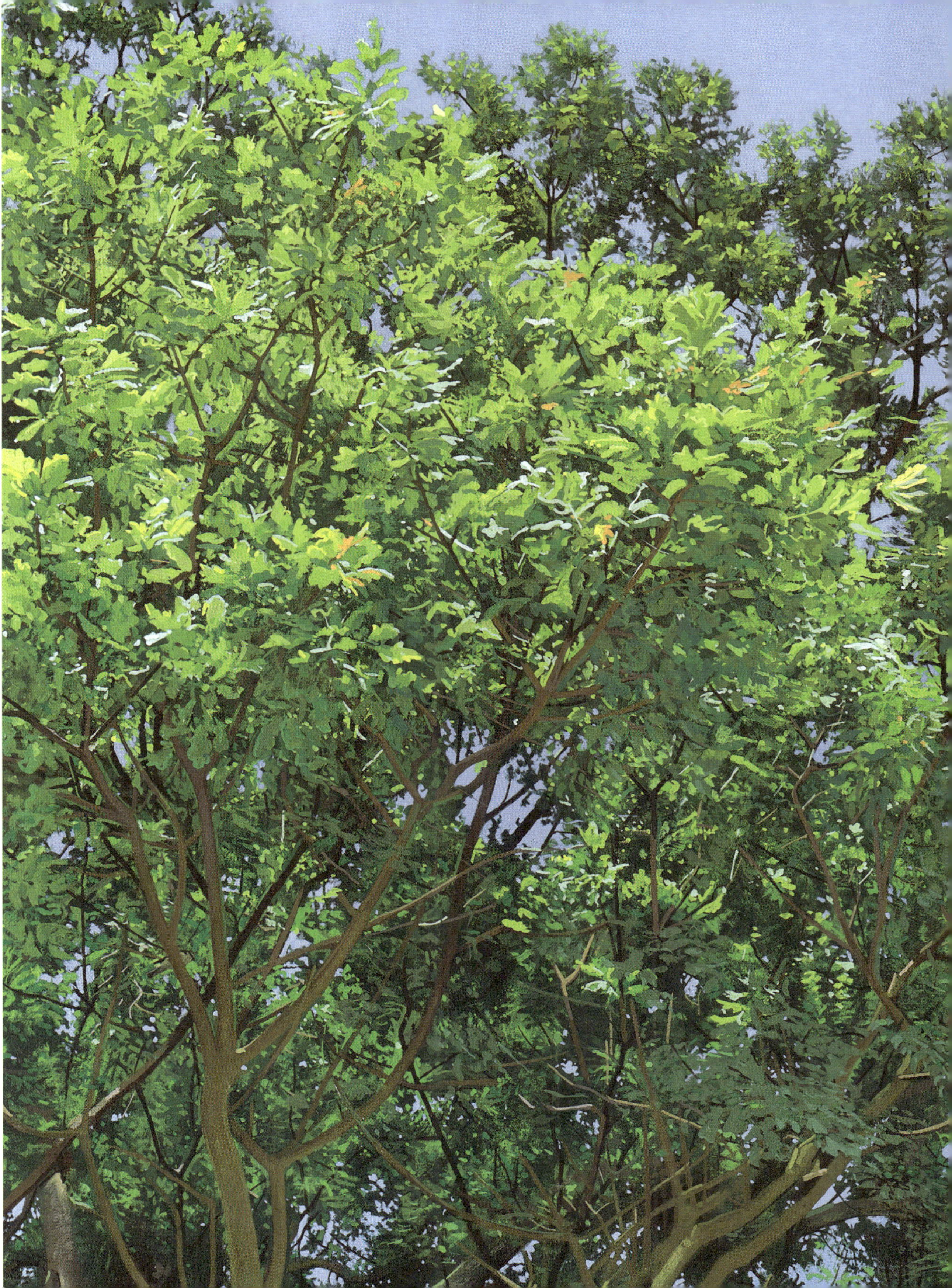

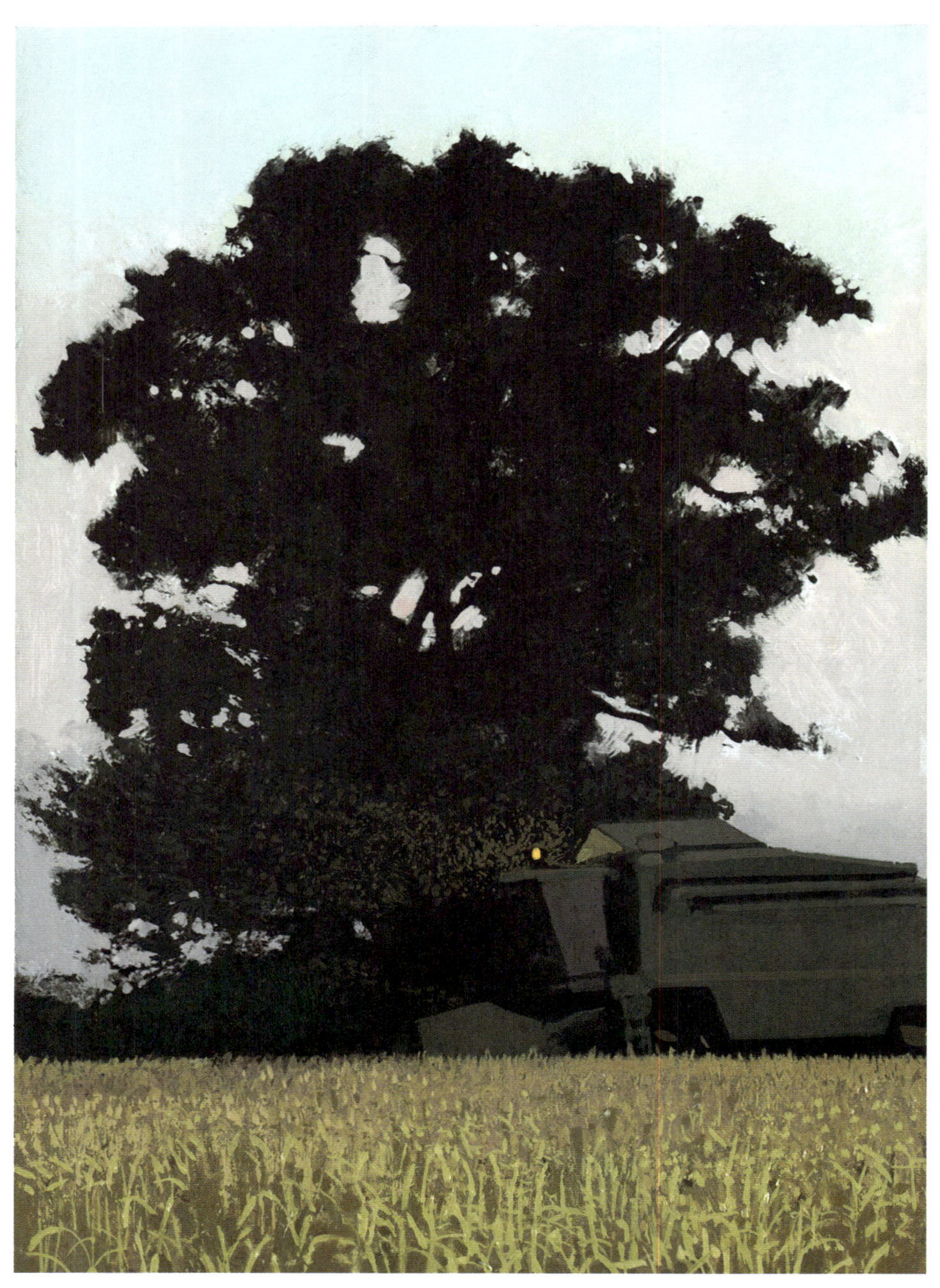

Reg Harvesting Barley. Oil on board, 183 mm x 130 mm.

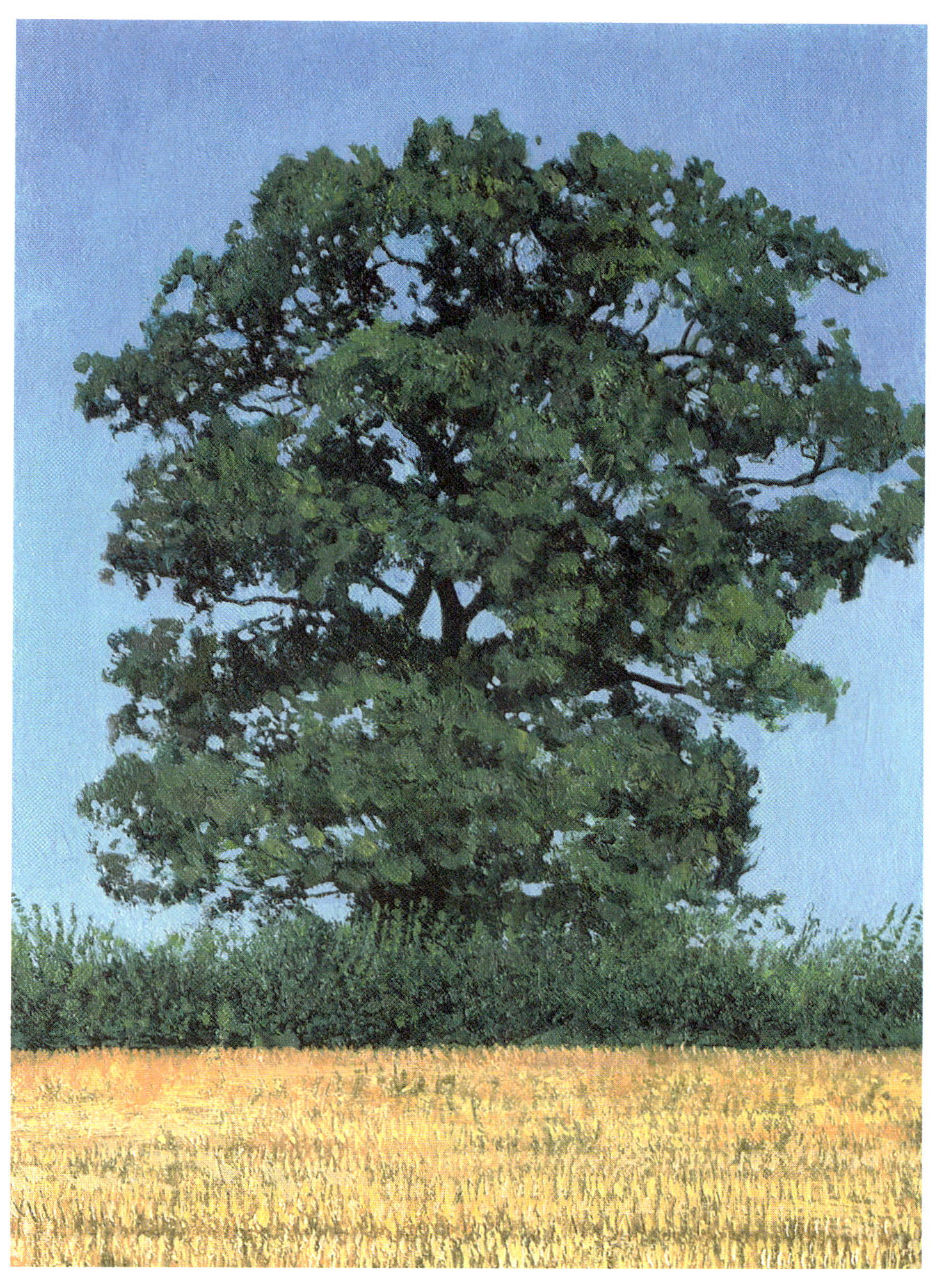

Barley Stubble. Oil on boarc, 183 mm x 130 mm.

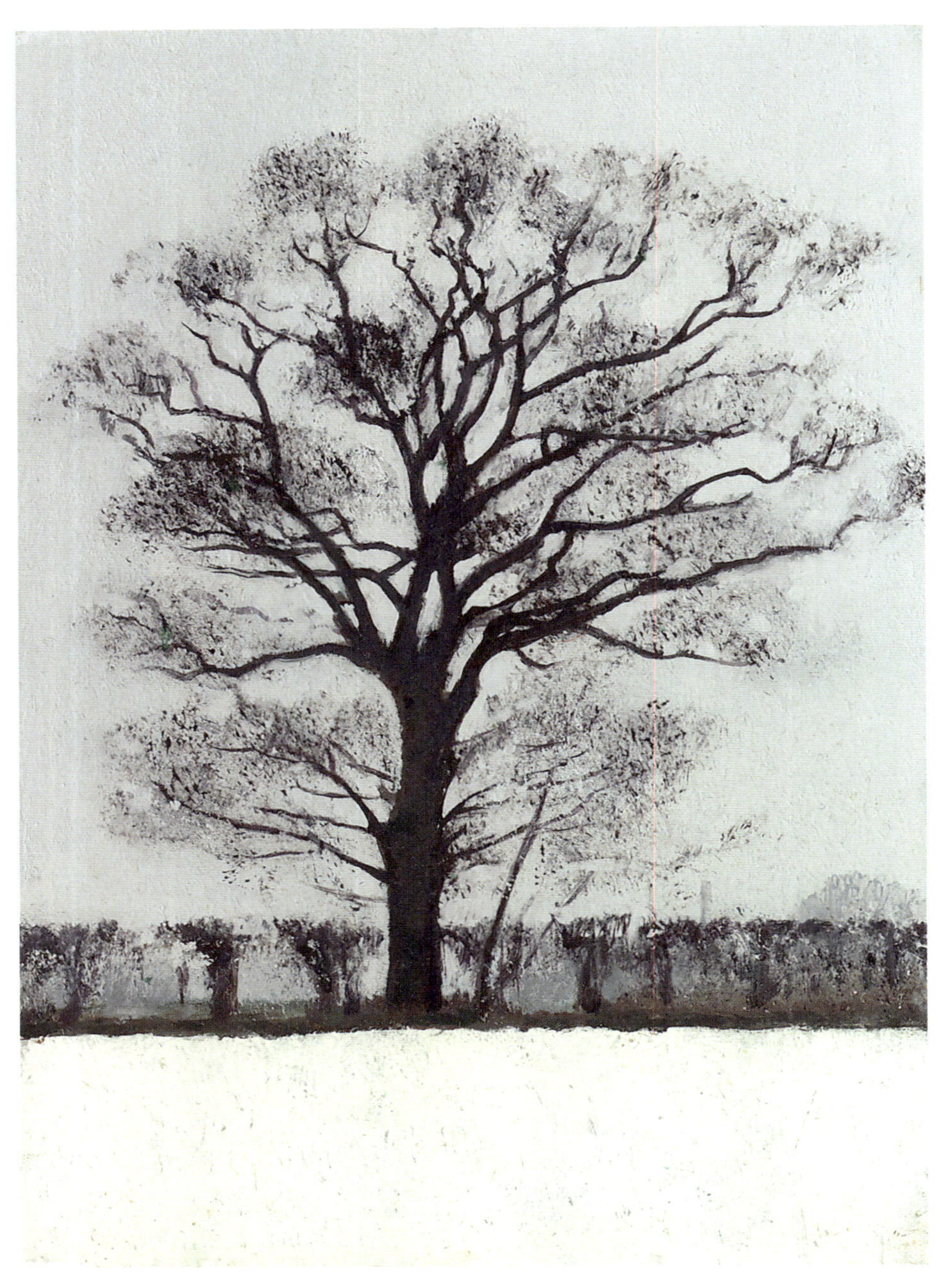

Blanket. Oil on board, 183 mm x 130 mm.

Only once was I driven back from my post by the weather. There was a severe snowstorm, and the oncoming snow was coming down as streams of dark dots against the sky but vanishing against the land. Big fragments loomed and smashed against my jacket. If you could paint this! But I couldn't paint in this weather—I could hardly walk in it. I went back the next day, after the storm, and painted this.

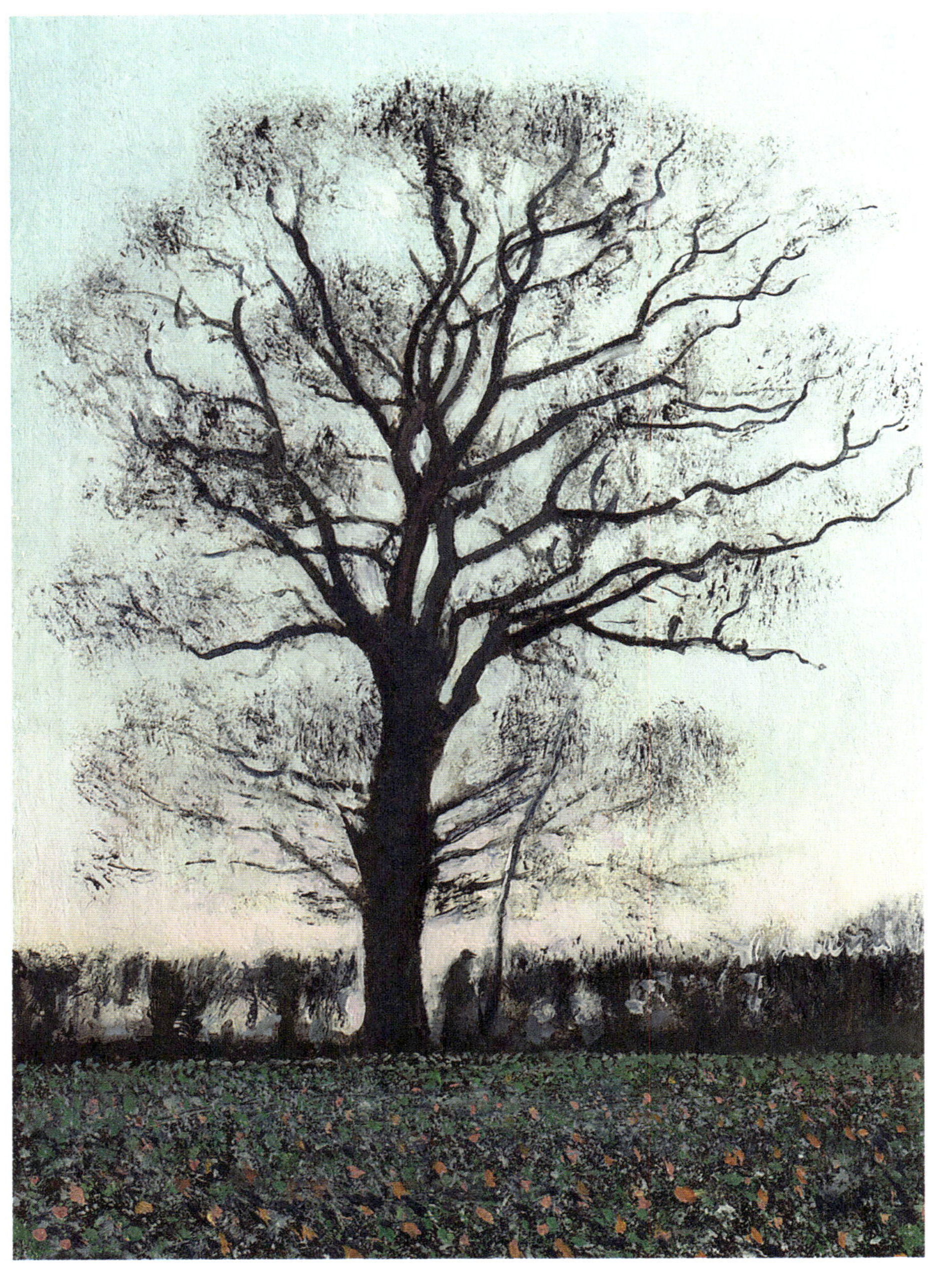

Man Walking Dog. Oil on board, 183 mm x 130 mm.

The crop rotation has come full circle and returned to rape, the crop that was in the field when I started painting the oak tree, three years earlier. Rape seedlings often have reddish leaves, a surprising colour in the English winter.

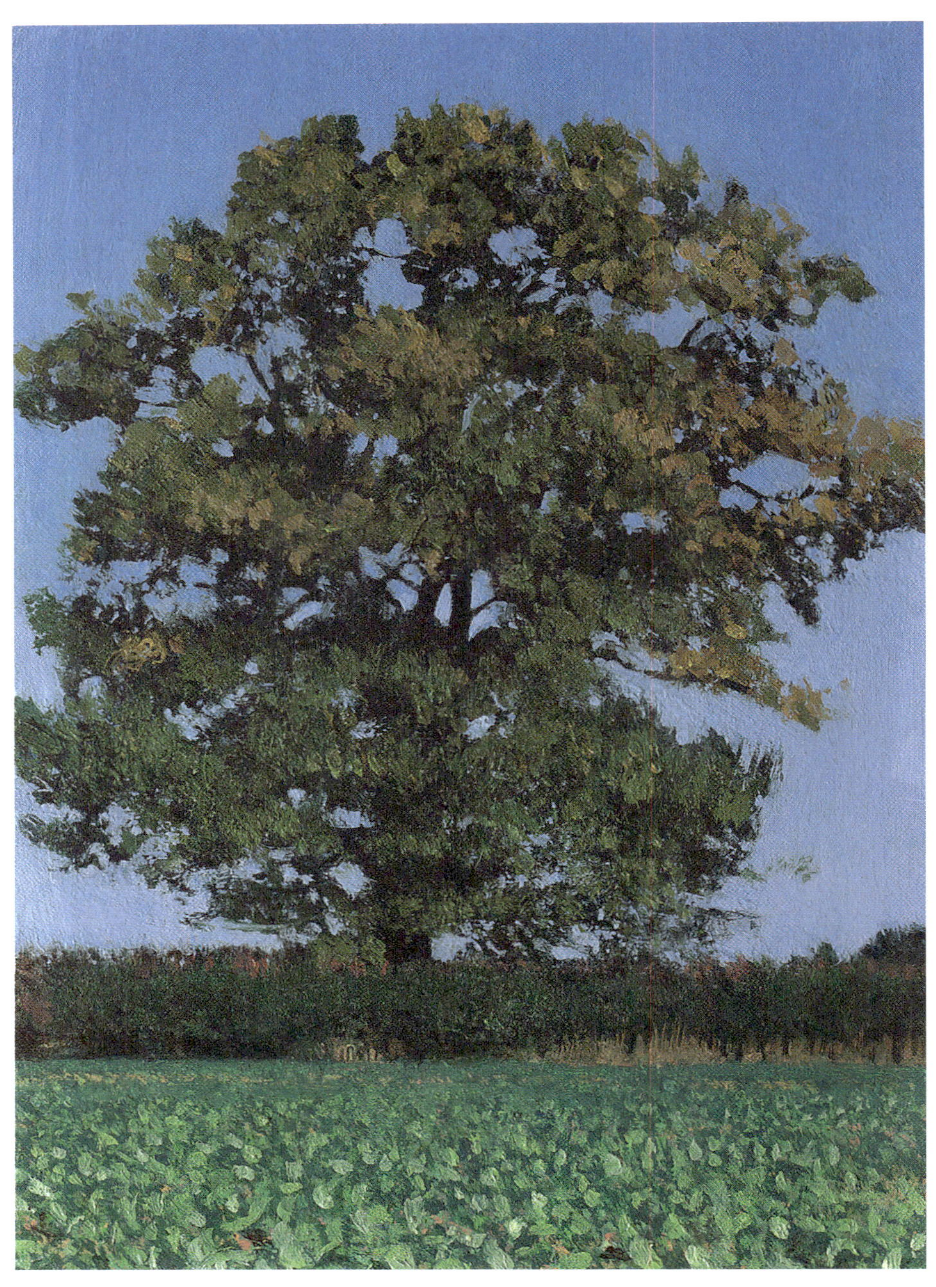

Rape Seedlings. Oil on board, 183 mm x 130 mm.

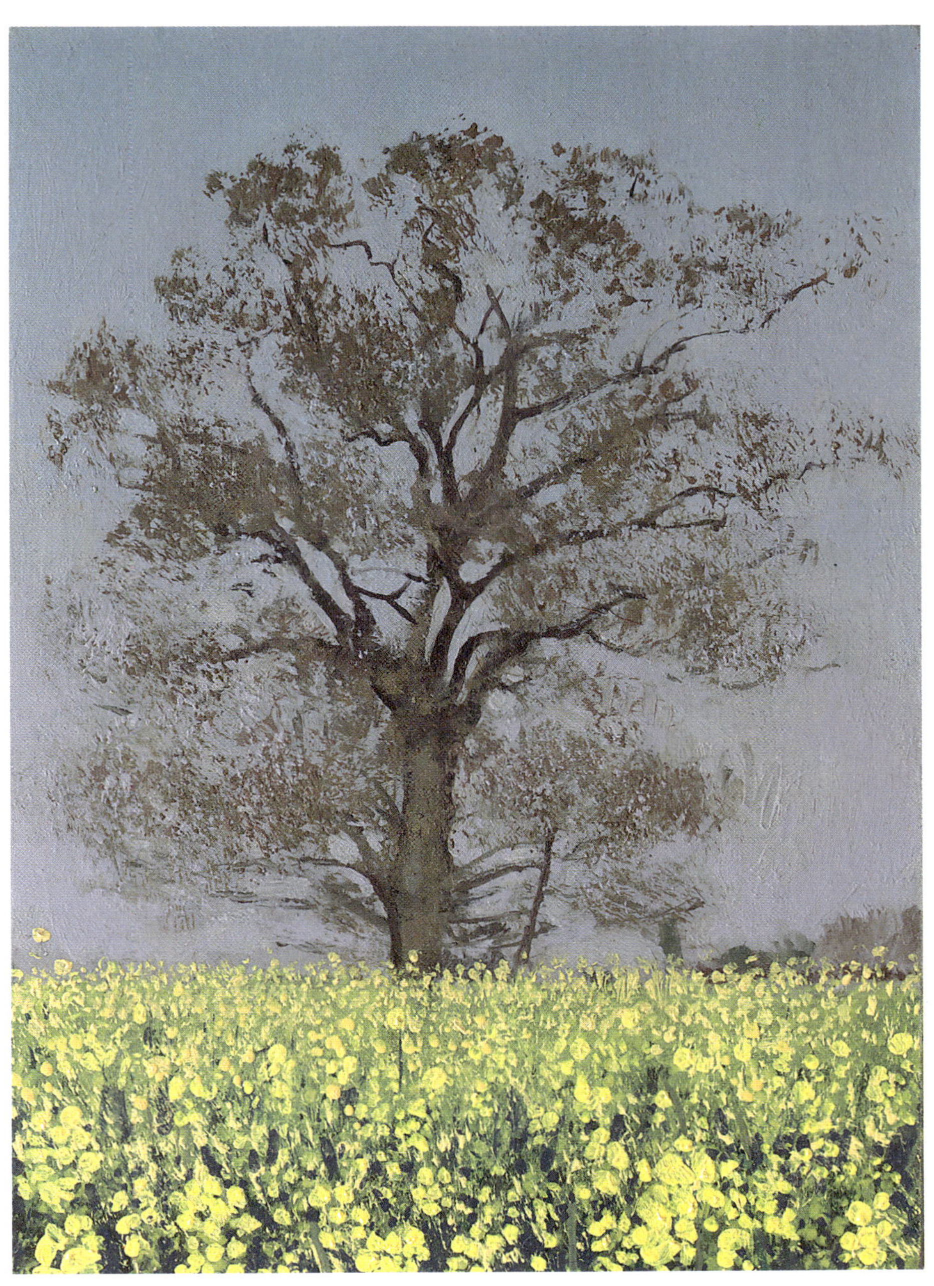

Oilseed Rape for Petrol. Oil on board, 183 mm x 130 mm.

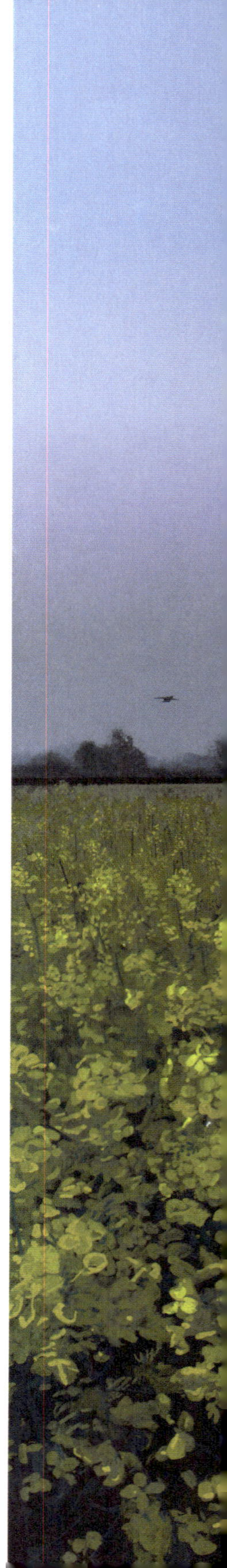

Swallows at 9pm. Oil on canvas, 1020 mm x 1020 mm.

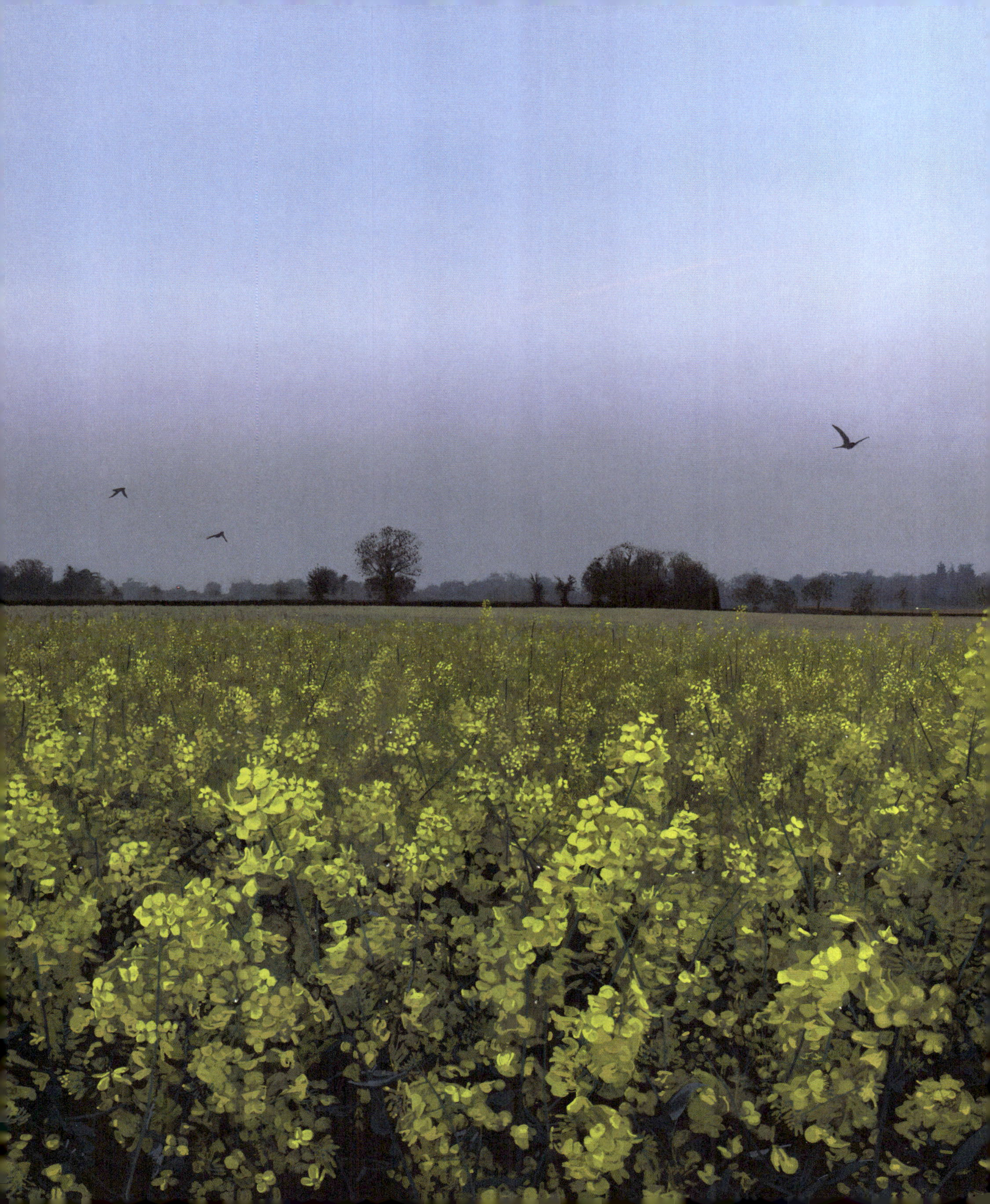

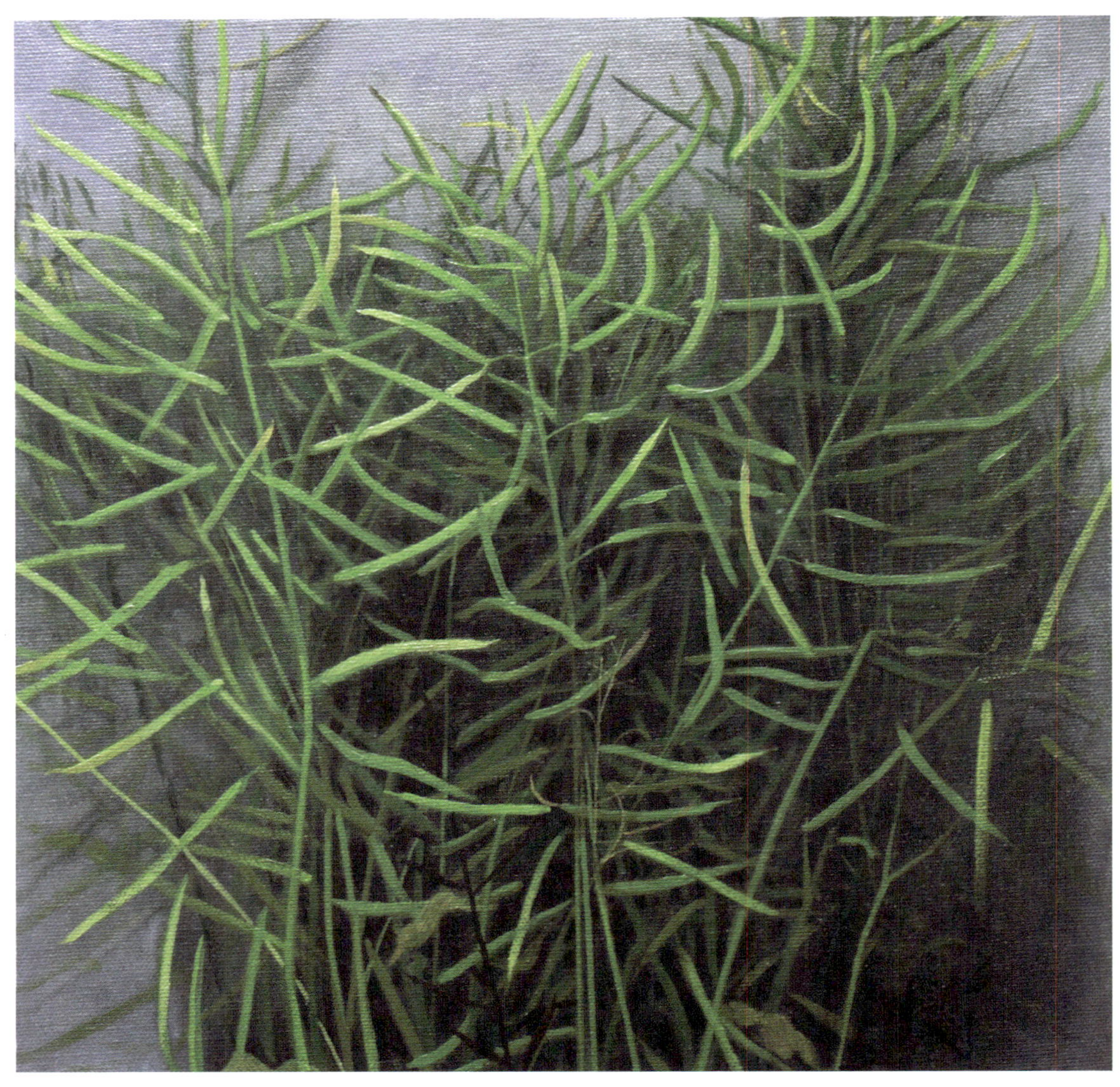

Oilseed Rape (Lioness). Oil on canvas, 300 mm x 300 mm.
Although the oak has long been native to England, the crops in the paintings
are all new varieties developed for modern, industrial-scale farming. Lioness
is a winter-sown conventional, as opposed to hybrid, variety of oilseed rape
developed in Germany.

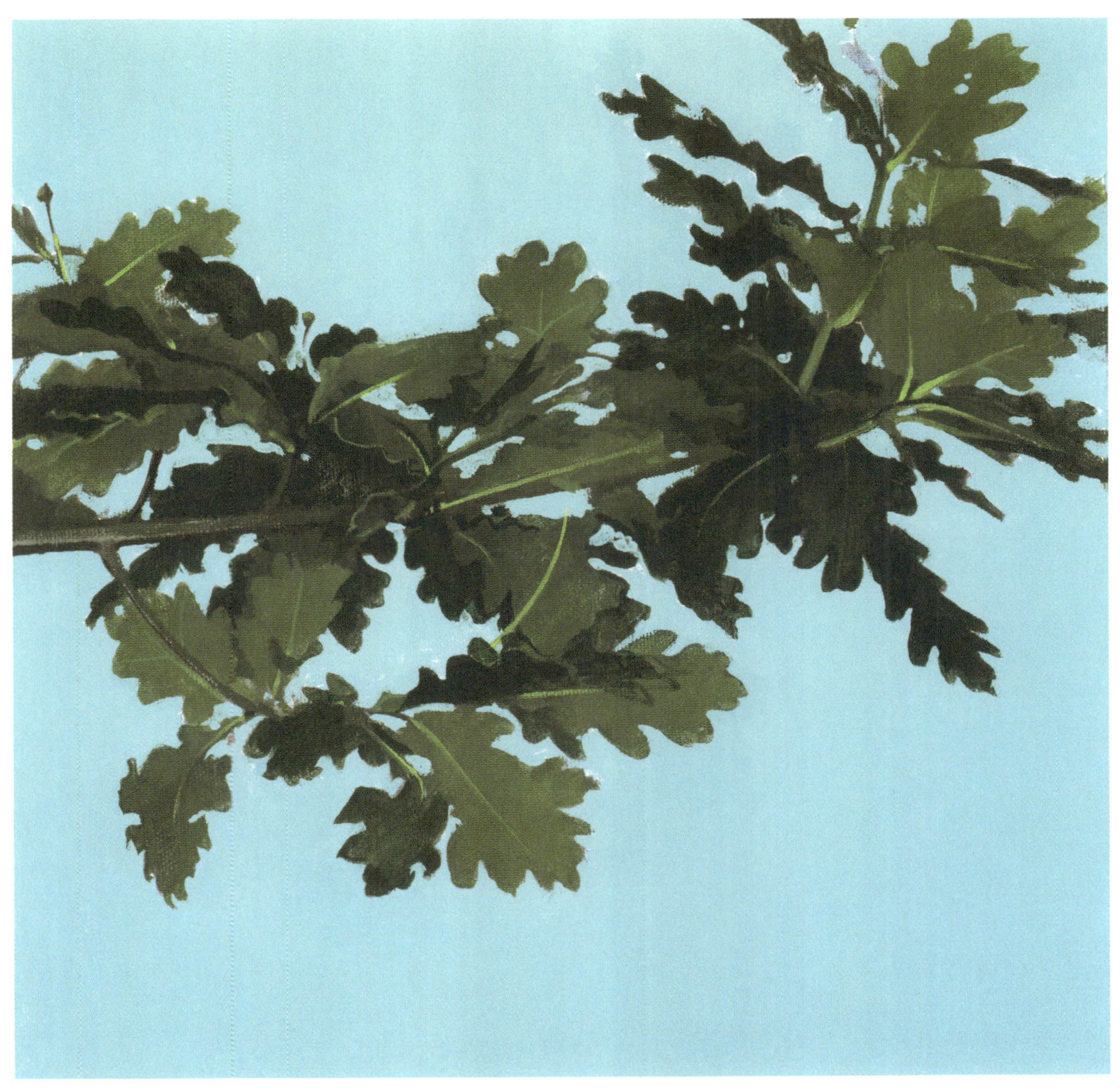

Oak Leaf Greens. Oil on canvas, 300 mm x 300 mm.
The two sides of oak leaves are different colours: a waxy cuticle seals the top, which is darker, to prevent uncontrolled loss of water by evaporation; the underside has open pores (stomata) that control water loss and carbon dioxide change. That is why oak trees appear to change colour in the wind.

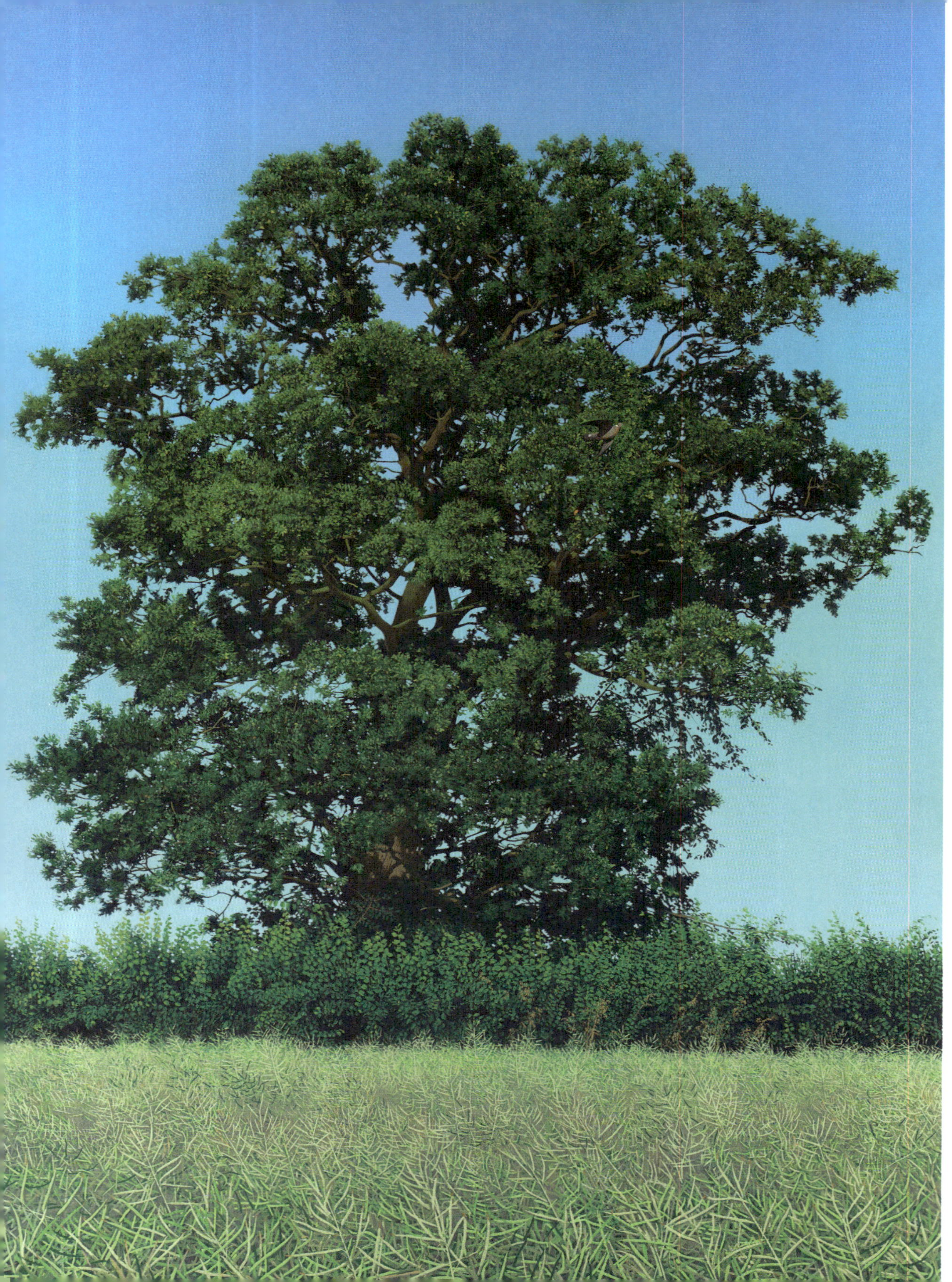

Wood Pigeon Flying over Oilseed Rape. Oil on canvas, 1550 mm x 1150 mm.
As you move toward a tree, more and more subtleties of colour become
visib e until every shade of green seems different from its neighbour.
The colours for this painting were taken from oil studies made close
to th tree. The overall shape of the tree is based on a view from
a distance, where it is easier to appreciate the general form. The
result is an image with a simple initial effect, like a sign, but with a
very wide range of colours. I wanted to make an oak tree that felt
both observed and imagined: an emblem embedded in vision.

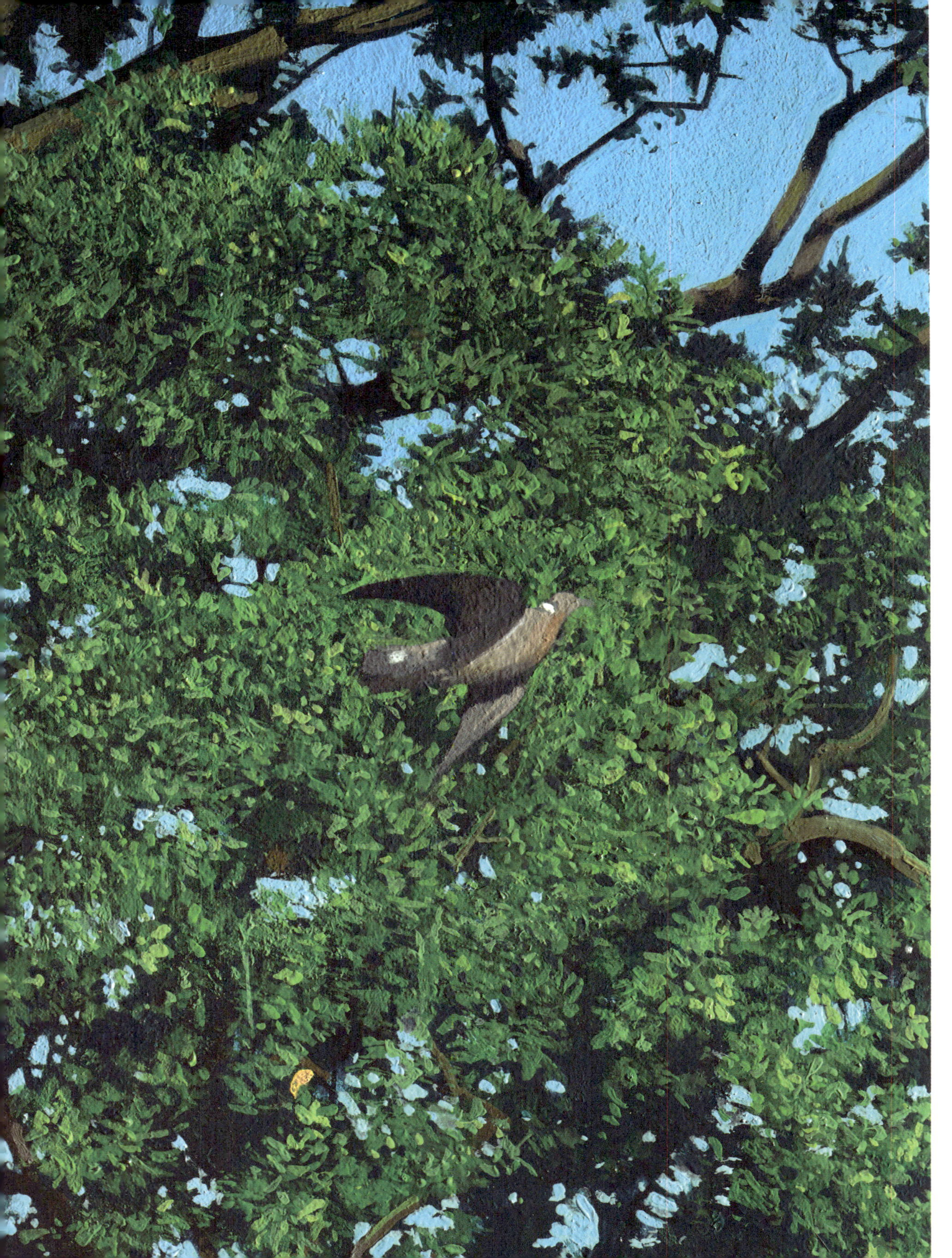

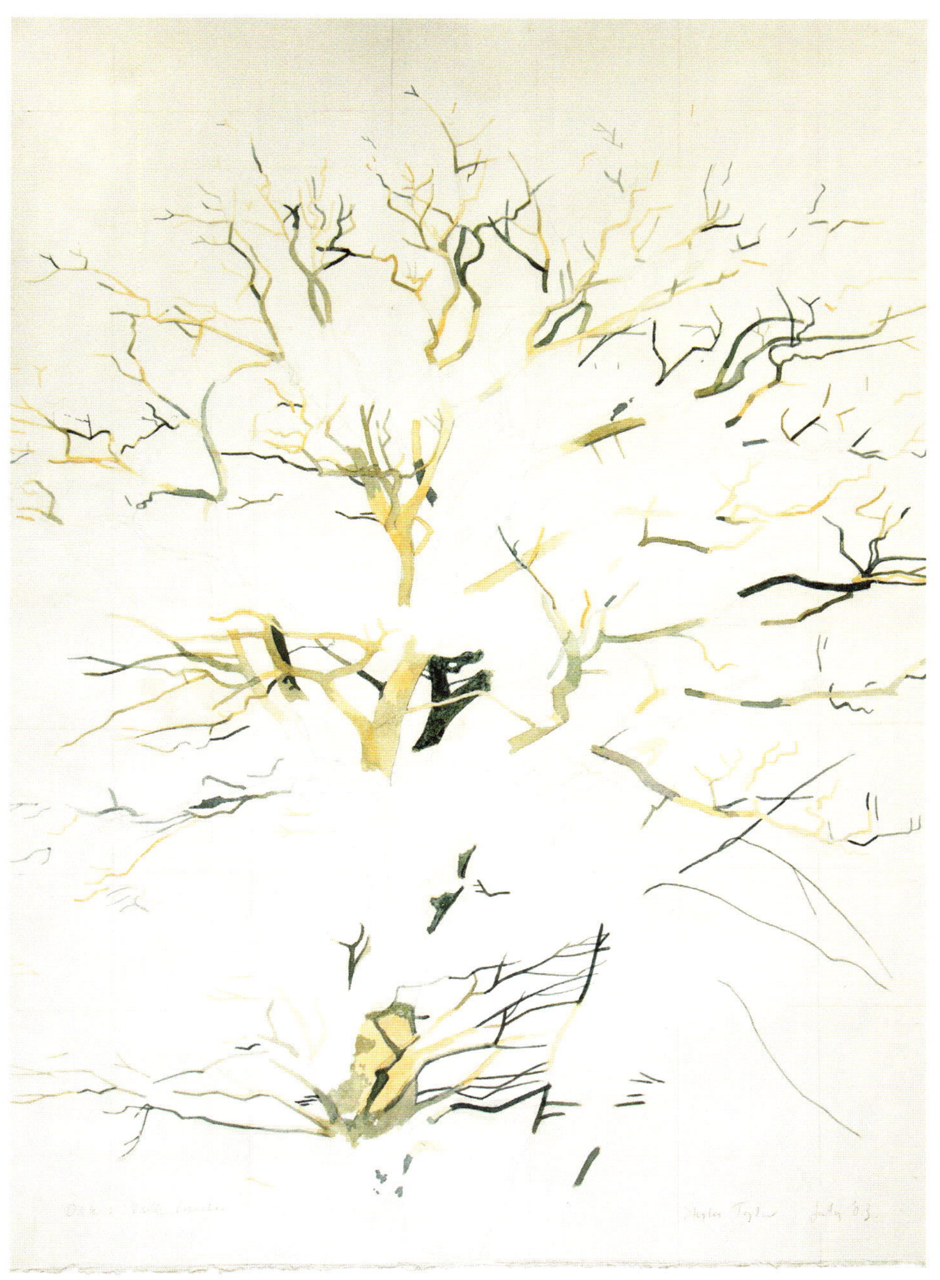

Visible Branches. Pencil, gouache, and watercolour on paper, 760 mm x 560 mm.

Study of branches visible within the tree when it was in full leaf.

Opposite: *Wood Pigeon Flying over Oilseed Rape*, detail.

Overleaf: *Wood Pigeon Flying over Oilseed Rape*, detail.

A screen of hazel below the architecture of the oak in full leaf.

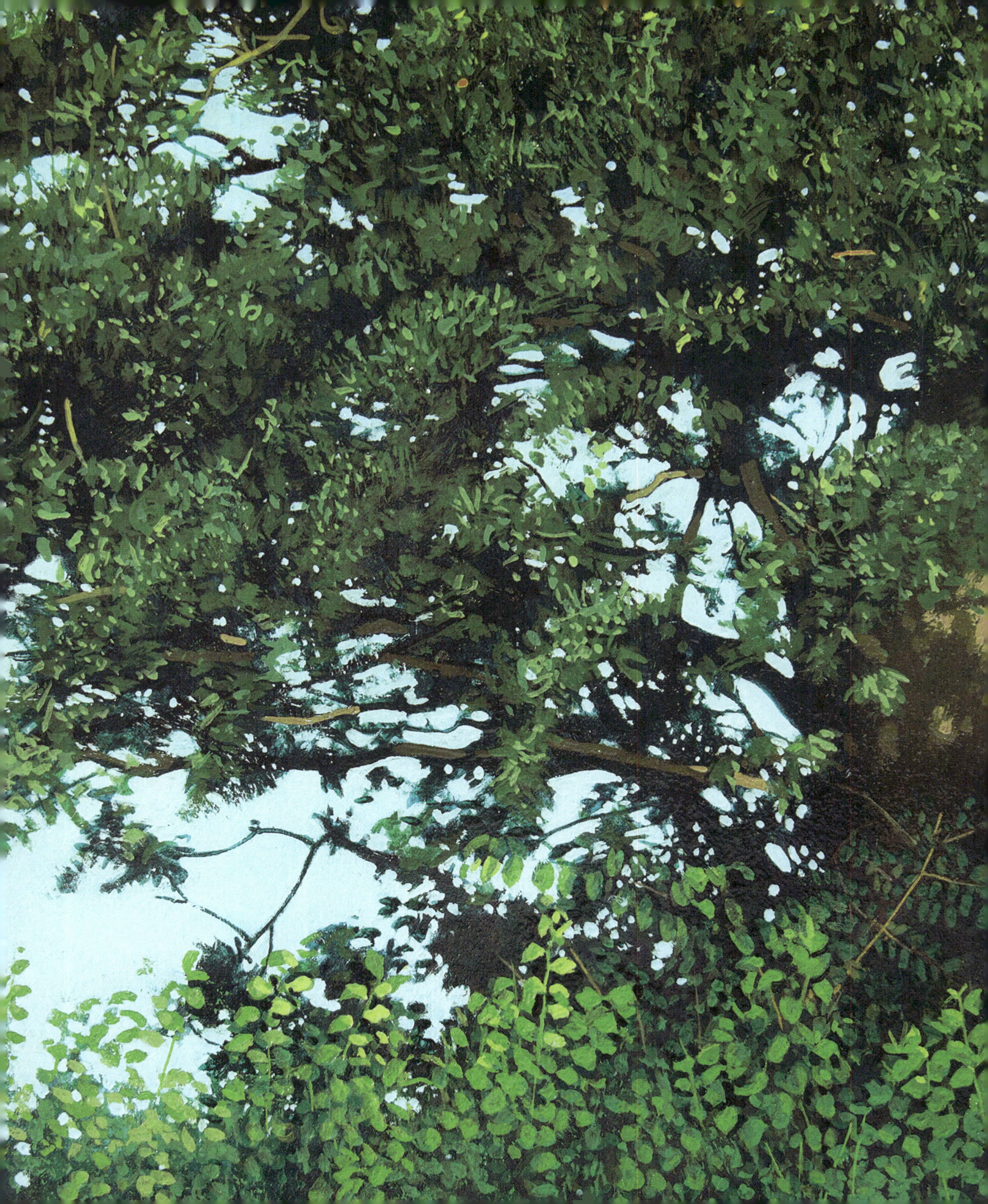

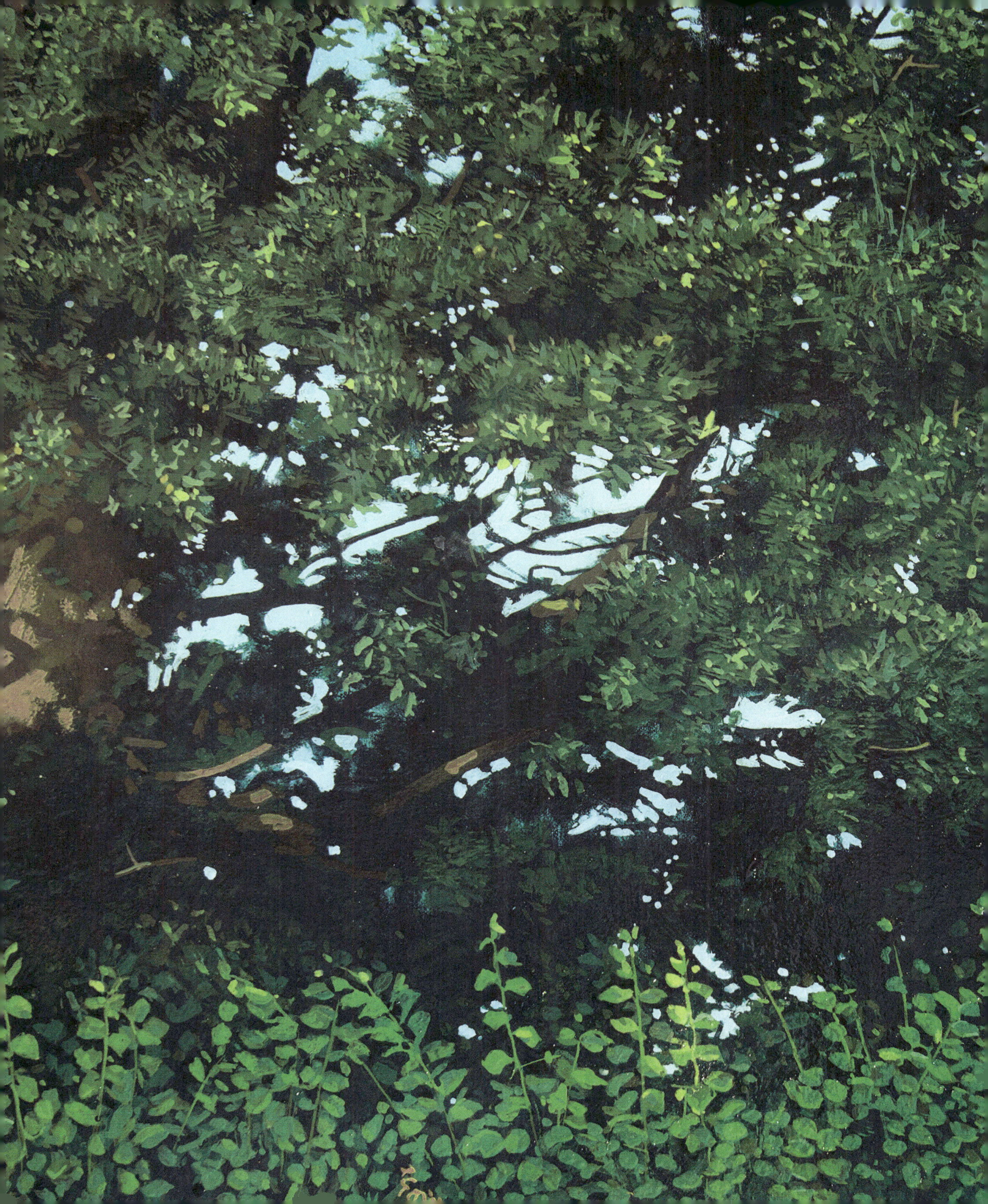

Semipermeable Membrane Series

This set of eight pictures was inspired by some cigarette cards from the 1930s that belonged to my father. The cards had pictures of British wild birds on one side and snippets of information from natural history or science, or even poetry about the bird, on the other. It seemed to me that we all have fragments from different fields of knowledge in our minds, so these little cards show how we think about nature.

The pictures on cards were rich in colour and detail—so rich that words could not possibly capture everything that was there. Images play an important role in drawing our attention to nature. An image with writing could be even more effective—I would make some paintings using both image and text. (See page 96.)

The title of the work is inspired by an idea in naturalist Richard Mabey's book *Nature Cure* (2005), in which he writes, "I believe that language and imagination, far from alienating us from nature, are our most powerful and natural tools for re-engaging with it.…Culture isn't the opposite or contrary of nature. It's the interface between us and the non-human world, our species' semipermeable membrane." I think the same can be said for painting.

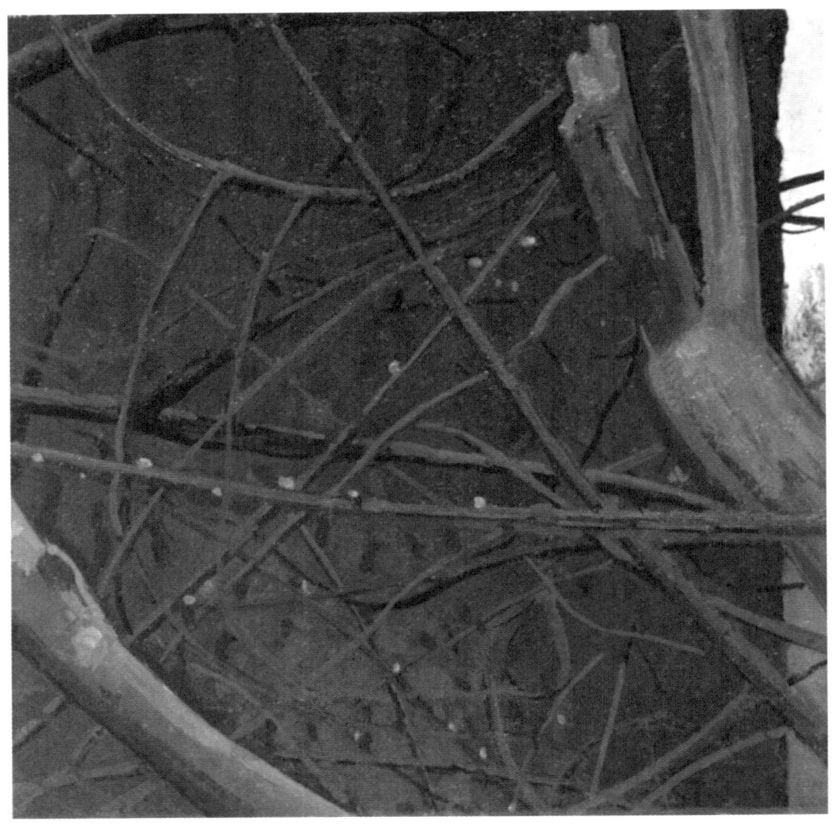

1. *Elm Sapling and Algae.* Oil on board, 100 mm x 100 mm.
The rich green of the oak bark is caused by algae that thrive on the side of
the tree most exposed to rain. The high acid content on that side prevents the
growth of lichen that would otherwise turn the bark grey. Hazel and elm buds
are just breaking in early April.

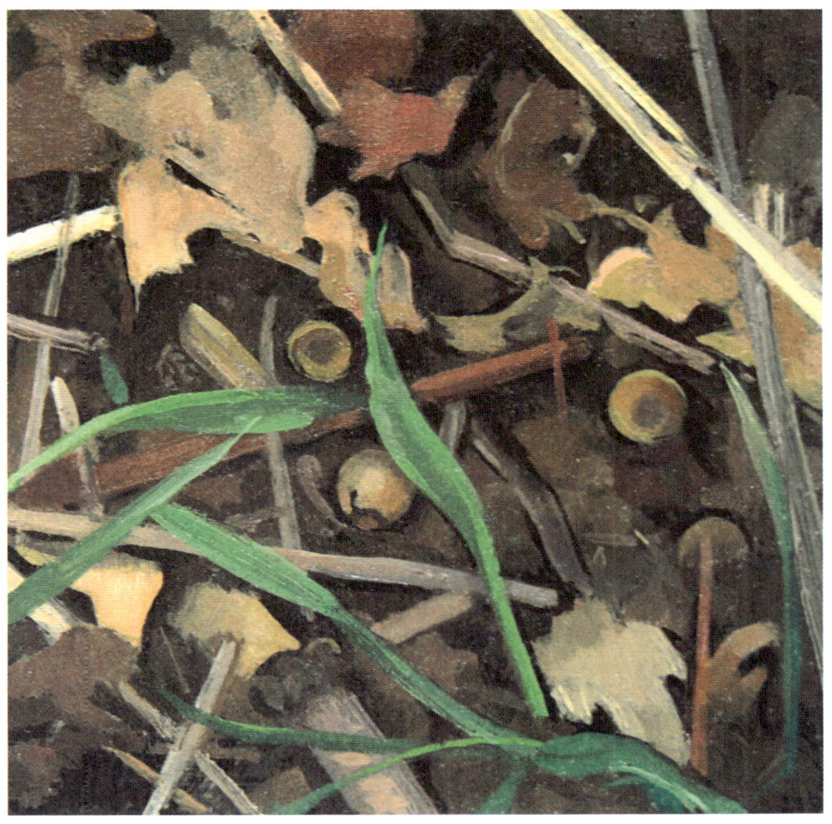

2. *Winter Litter.* Oil on board, 100 mm x 100 mm.

Between October and December many leaves shed onto the woodland floor.
By March only one-third of the fallen leaves remains—the rest has been
eaten. Each square metre contains millions of bacteria as well as mites,
springtails, amoebae, rotifers, eelworms, earthworms, millipedes, false
scorpions, slugs, and snails. The hole in the acorn (at centre) is the exit hole
of a weevil, whose larva feed internally on the healthy, living acorn.

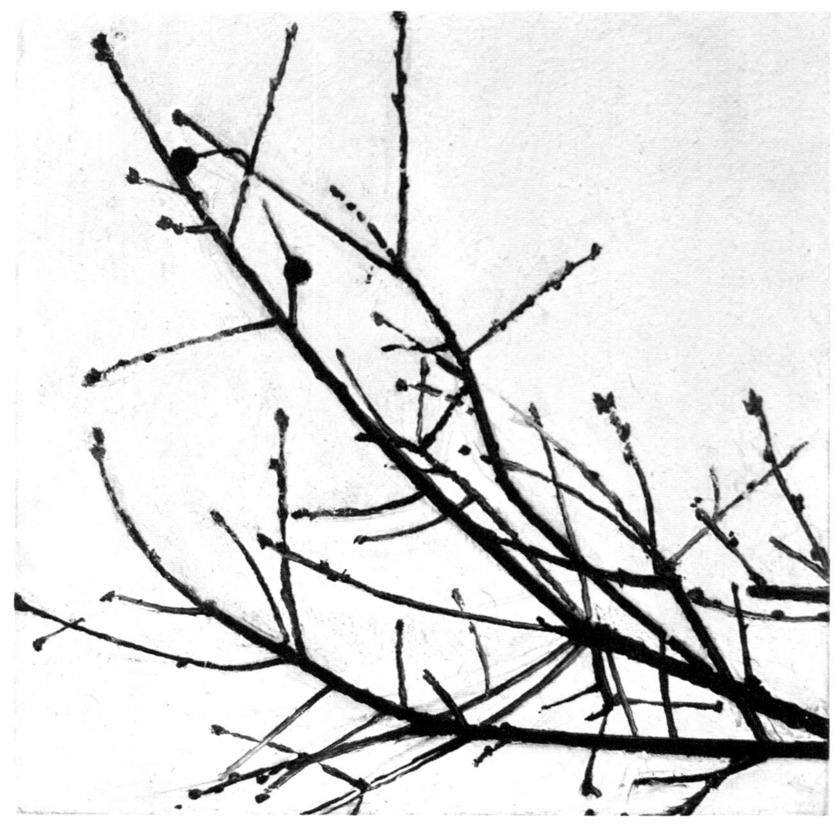

3. *Twigs.* Oil on board, 100 mm x 100 mm.

The acorn cups remain on the end of long stalks. These stalks are a
distinguishing feature of the common oak, as opposed to the sessile
oak, whose acorns are tight against the twigs. (The Latin *sessilis* means
"stalkless.") The common oak is ubiquitous in Britain, while the often
smaller sessile oak is usually found in wetter, often windy uplands in the
north and west of Britain.

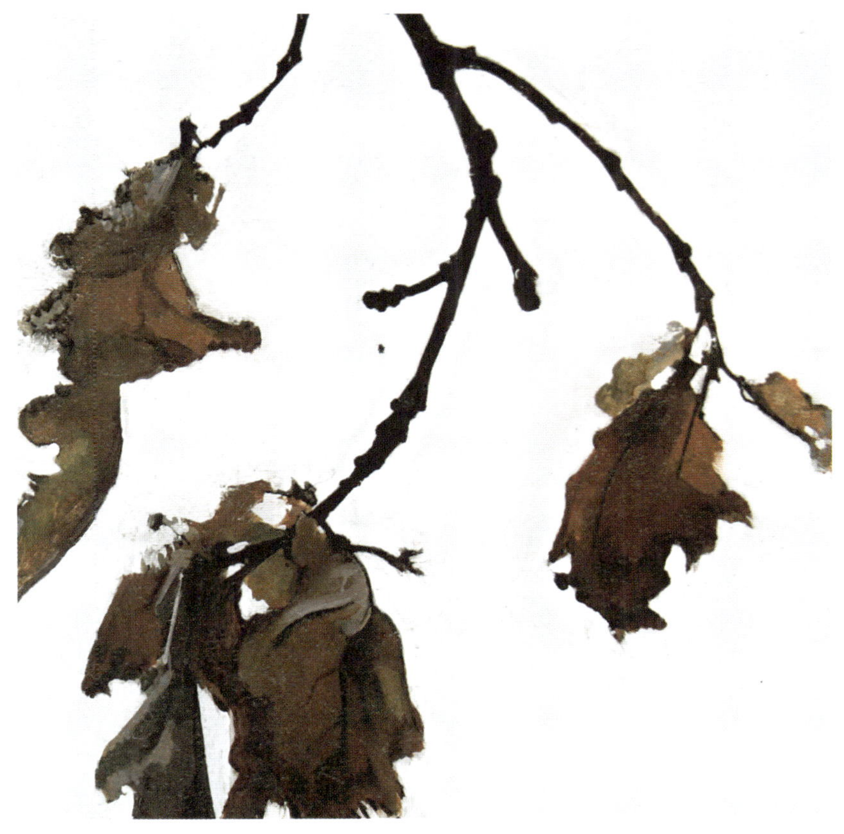

4. *Unfallen Leaves.* Oil on board, 100 mm x 100 mm.

If a branch breaks or falls, the attached leaves often stay on the branch.
In March these leaves were still joined to a broken branch, decaying in the
air. Light transmitted through the leaves shows the bright orange pigments
normally associated with autumn.

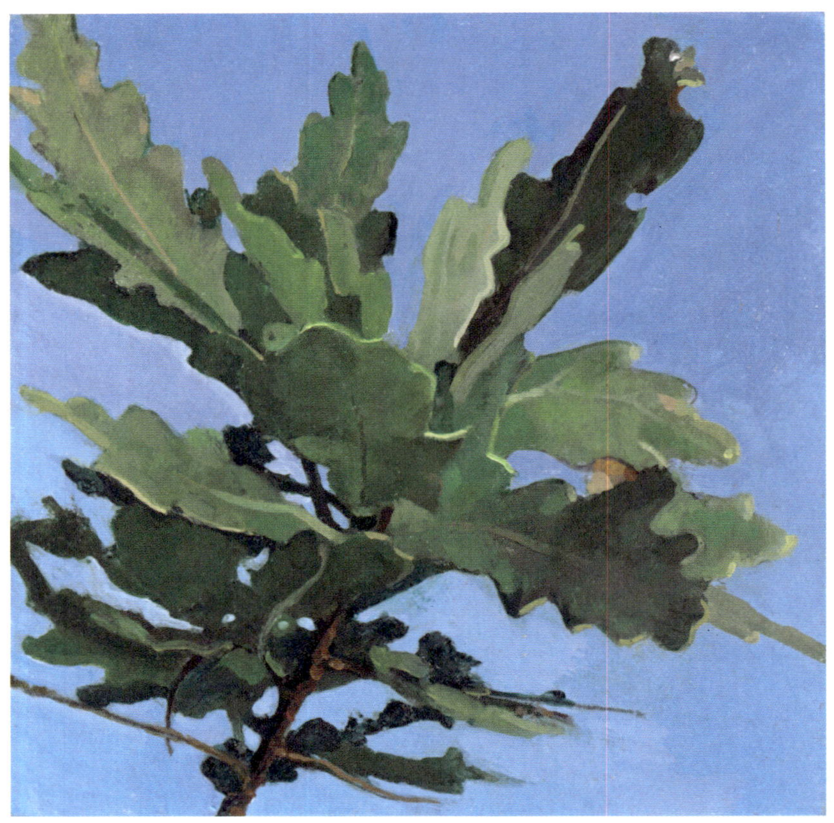

5. *Lammas Leaves.* Oil on board, 100 mm x 100 mm.

The olive leaves are new summer "lammas" leaves growing on the tree to supplement the leaves of spring that have been eaten by the insects that live on the oak. The new leaves are often reddish in hue and vary in size. Summer sunlight falling on these leaves makes the whole tree look the same bright pale green as it did in early spring. (Lammas Day, August 1st, was an old English feast day, celebrating the wheat harvest. The replacement leaves appear on the oak at this time of year, hence the name lammas leaves.)

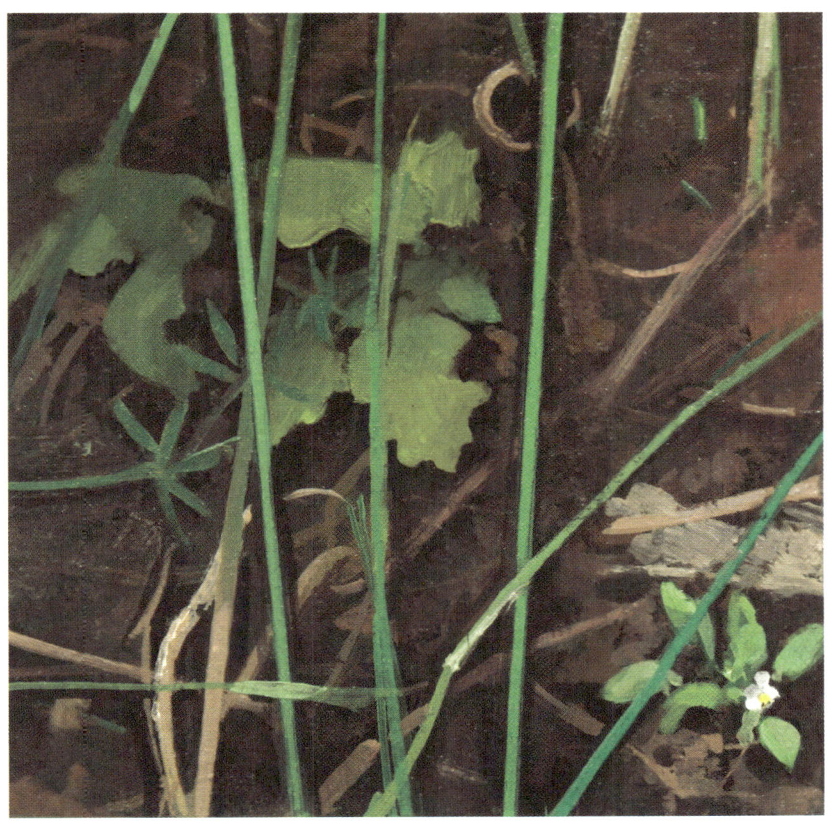

6. *Oak Seedling*. Oil on board, 100 mm x 100 mm.

An oak seedling at the foot of the tree has survived through winter and extends its leaves during its second or third year. The seedling has already laid down a layer of wood, the first of many tree rings. The plant to the left with a starlike leaf pattern is called sticky willie because of its small green fruits with hooked bristles that stick to clothes and is also known as cleavers or goosegrass. The plant at the bottom right is a field pansy.

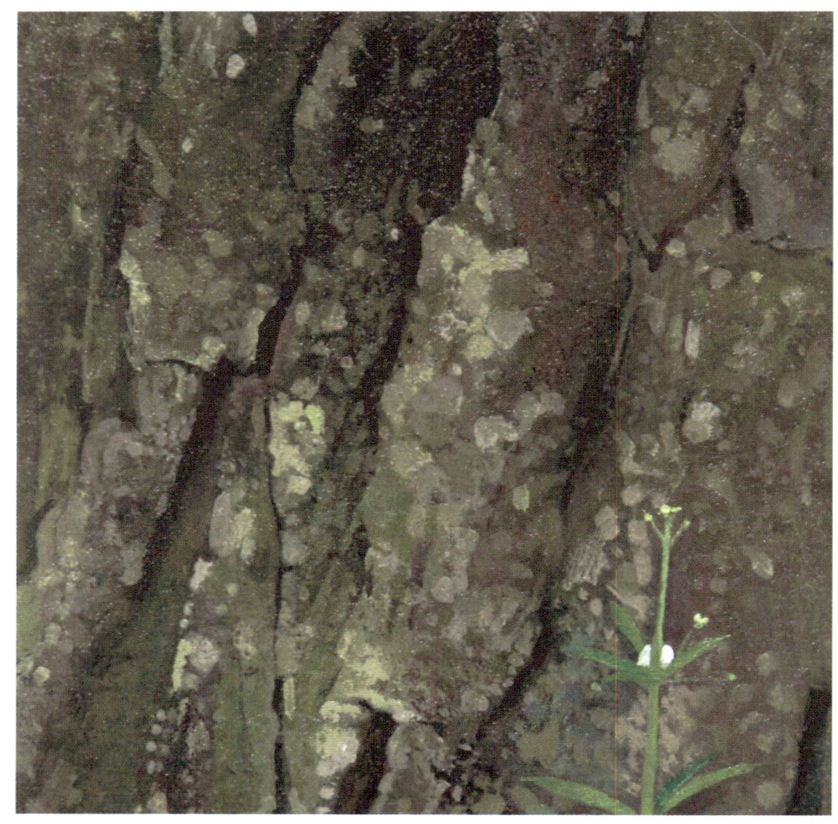

7. *Bark and Lichens.* Oil on board, 100 mm x 100 mm.

Lichens are composite organisms made of fungi and algae. Like moss they are epiphytes, which grow upon something else without feeding on it. The lichen visible on this bark grows on the relatively sheltered north side of the trunk, away from rain. A sticky willie is at the bottom right. The whitish blobs are clumps of cuckoo spit, a frothy viscous secretion of froghopper bugs, which protects them from desiccation and predators while they suck the plant's sap.

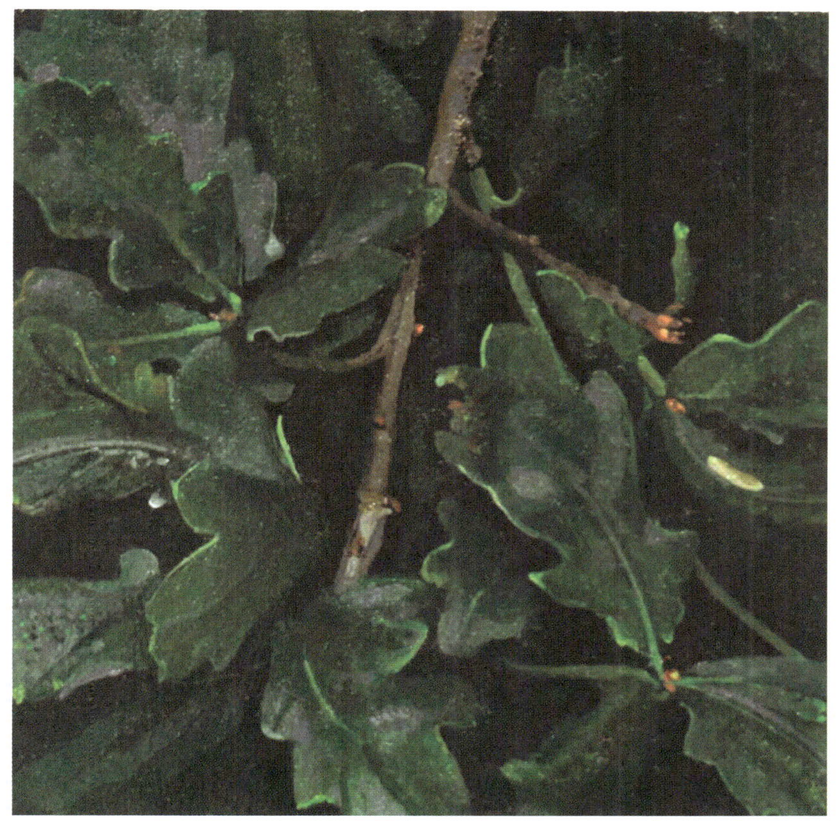

8. *Summer Leaves*. Oil on board, 100 mm x 100 mm.

Summer leaves attract many and varied insects. Throughout the course of its life, the common oak supports five hundred species of invertebrates, more than any other species of British tree. The leaves are eaten from the outside and from within. The tip of the bud at the top right has been eaten before it was able to open its leaves. Below it, to its right, is a pale, oblong chamber made by a moth caterpillar as it incubates inside the leaf.

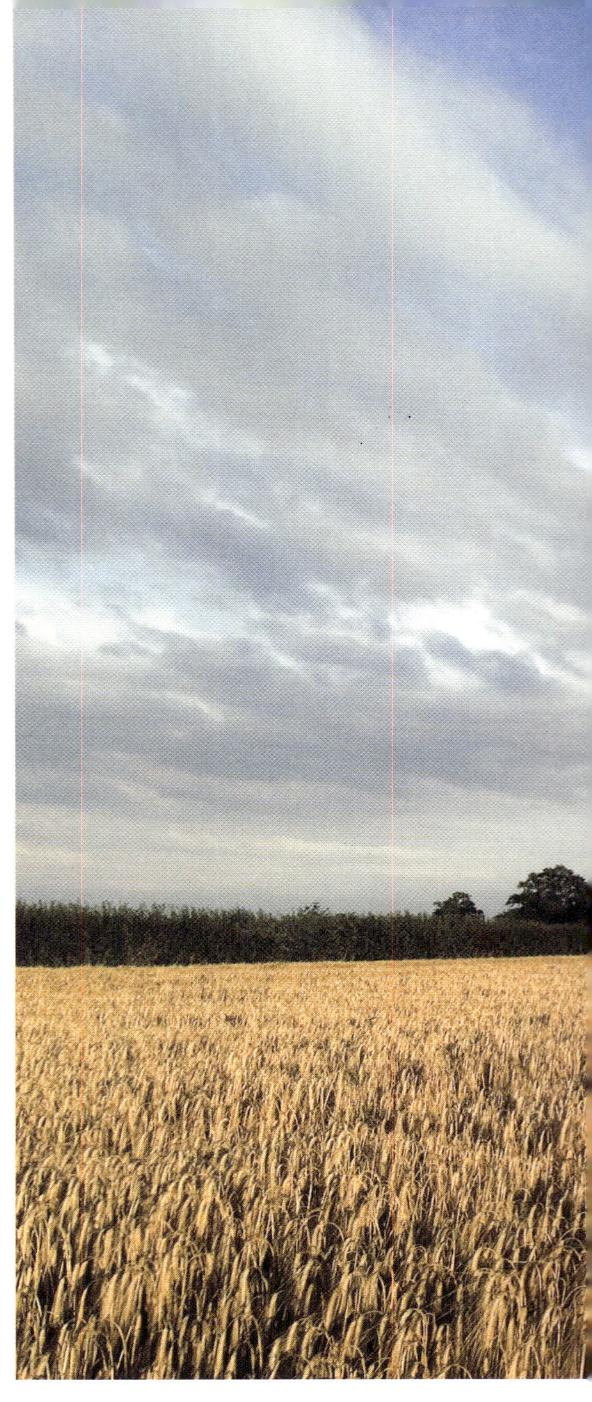

Author walking to work

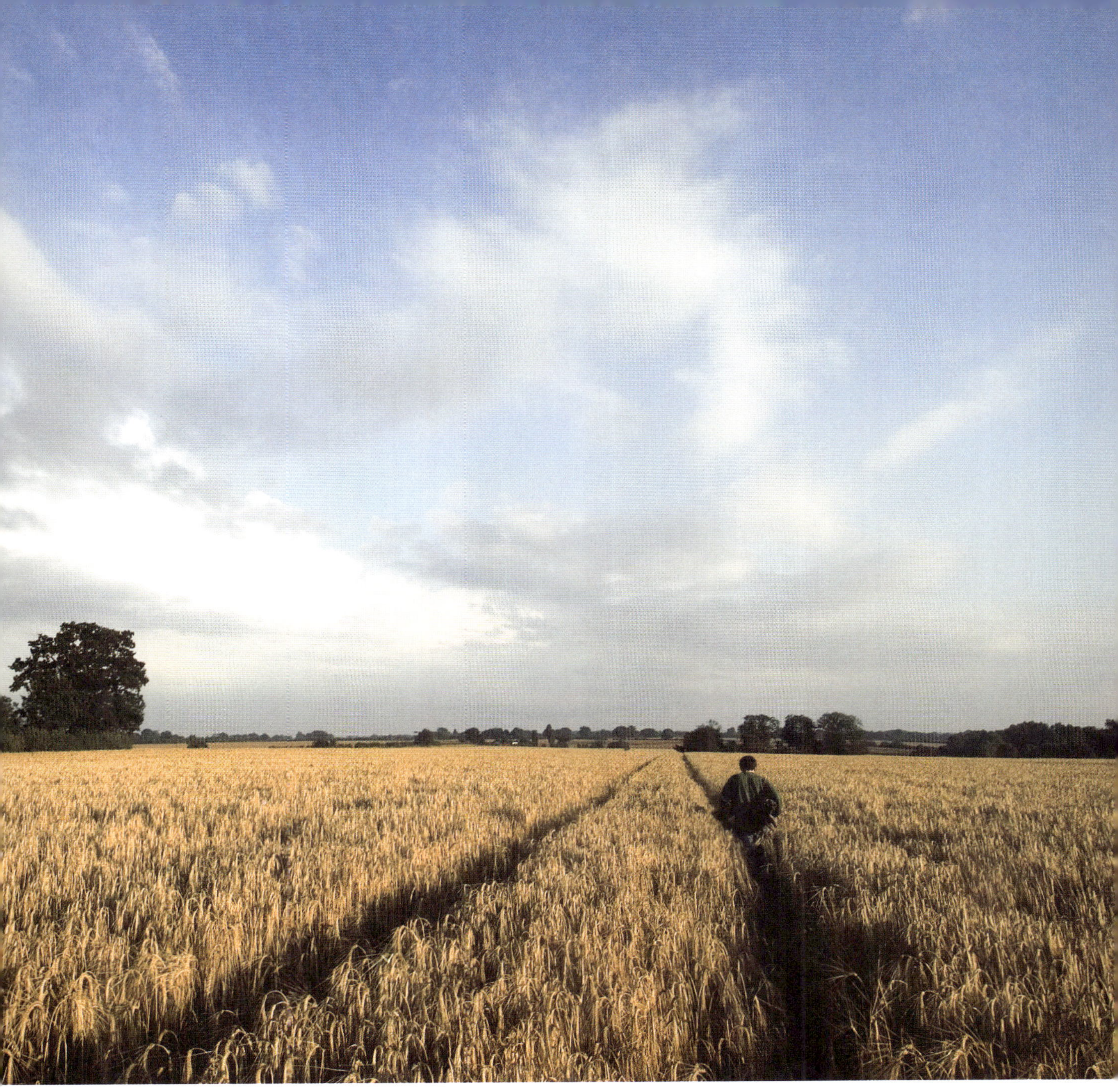

From Start to Finish:
Making an Oak Tree Painting

STARTING POINTS

The natural world is visually very rich and constantly changing. From light reflecting on a mountain stream to the pattern of fallen leaves in a forest, nature is visually unpredictable and often very hard to see clearly. So I use painting to help me discover what is there. My methods are designed to clarify the complex colours and shapes I see. The approach is empirical, and I use science to help me observe. At the same time, a painting is more than a neutral record. My choice of colours is selective, and the picture expresses the associative and emotional concerns of the observer-painter. There are two sides to the way I work: one that takes place outdoors and another indoors. I trace the steps I took in creating *Swallows at 9pm* as a way to show my typical working process for a large painting. (See plates 13–15, pages 102–3.) Seeing a picture develop from start to finish should help to get closer to the painting and to see how it can be both observational and expressive at the same time.

OUTDOORS

Outside, everything I do is to help my senses and my reactions adjust to the natural world. I want my work to come out of an intimate connection with a place. By the time I came to paint *Swallows at 9pm*, I had been working in the same field for six years, so I was familiar with its character. Each picture is unique and requires its own set of adjustments: for an evening picture like this, I arrive early to let my eyes adapt.

I strapped a pochade box around my neck so I could work standing up in the crop, which was chest high at this time of the year, and I mounted a digital camera on a tripod. Figure 1 I had a canvas seat to rest on, as well as hot coffee, snacks, fruit, and a tot of whisky. I take an extra set of old clothes—even in summer I can get cold if I'm standing still. I probably look like a tramp. I remember feeling utterly happy at this point, with my brushes, palettes, and rags, just looking…

I sometimes use photographs—taken years, days, or just minutes before—as inspiration. You can shoot, evaluate, adjust, and reshoot digital shots on the spot. I do not always start colour studies with a photographic prompt, but I will take selective exposure shots as soon as I see the effect I'm after.

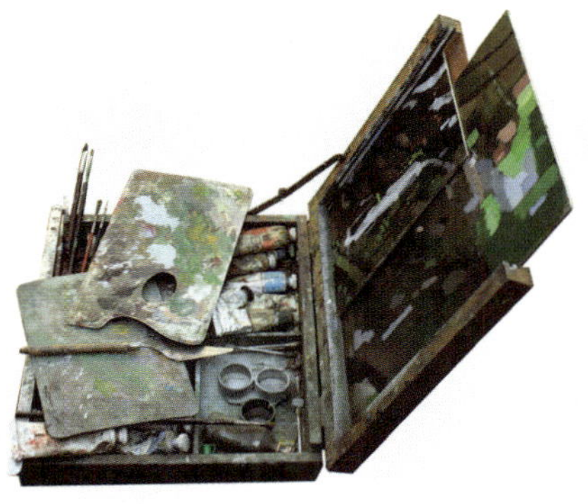

1 | A pochade (small sketch) box, developed in the nineteenth century to help painters work outdoors. The lid has slots for panels so that wet paintings can be transported without damage. There is a strap to permit the artist to paint standing up. Sitting down, the box rests on the lap. With a seat and an umbrella, it makes a small portable studio.

I had already taken photographs of the field of rape around six o'clock during a previous summer evening. (I had taken them because I felt that people don't really look at rape as it responds to sunlight.) I wanted to use the bright yellow of the industrial crop to create an extreme contrast with the delicate tones of the trees, so I would paint in the early evening, when sunlight has a reddish colour that makes the field look luminous.

I was set up under a clear sky, ready to go. I first put an approximate base key (a set of background colours that helps judge subsequent local colours more accurately than is possible on a white background) over the entire board using quick-drying acrylic. At six o'clock the crop started to catch the warm light of the setting sun, and I started to paint quickly in oil.

I make colour mixes in clear, definite values, each one based on what I see and carefully compared with the other colours around it. This exacting comparison and mixing is fundamental to observational painting and is something students need to practice. Each colour we perceive is effected by the colours surrounding it, and by analysing individual colours and their relationships to those around them, you can discover the unique character and lighting of a scene.[1] Each study is a form of empirical discovery—and also a race, because the faster the light changes, the faster you have to work.

When I lay down the main colours, I start with big areas first. But in this case, they did not seem to work together. The light was fading very slowly, so I waited for something different to happen. I sat down and prepared another board in a darker key for the lower light that would come.

As the sun set behind me, the shadow of the earth rose on the horizon, reversing the usual gradient so that the sky above became brighter than the lower sky, which passed into a grey limbo. The crop was now in shadow but still luminous; detail in the trees on the horizon began to fall away. I noticed new, unimaginable red-blue greens within the rape.

I worked fast and in under an hour had laid down all I needed. At the same time, I took a series of selectively exposed photos. It was about nine o'clock when a small group of swallows flew straight at and passed me like bullets. The lead bird looked violet against the rape. I rapidly

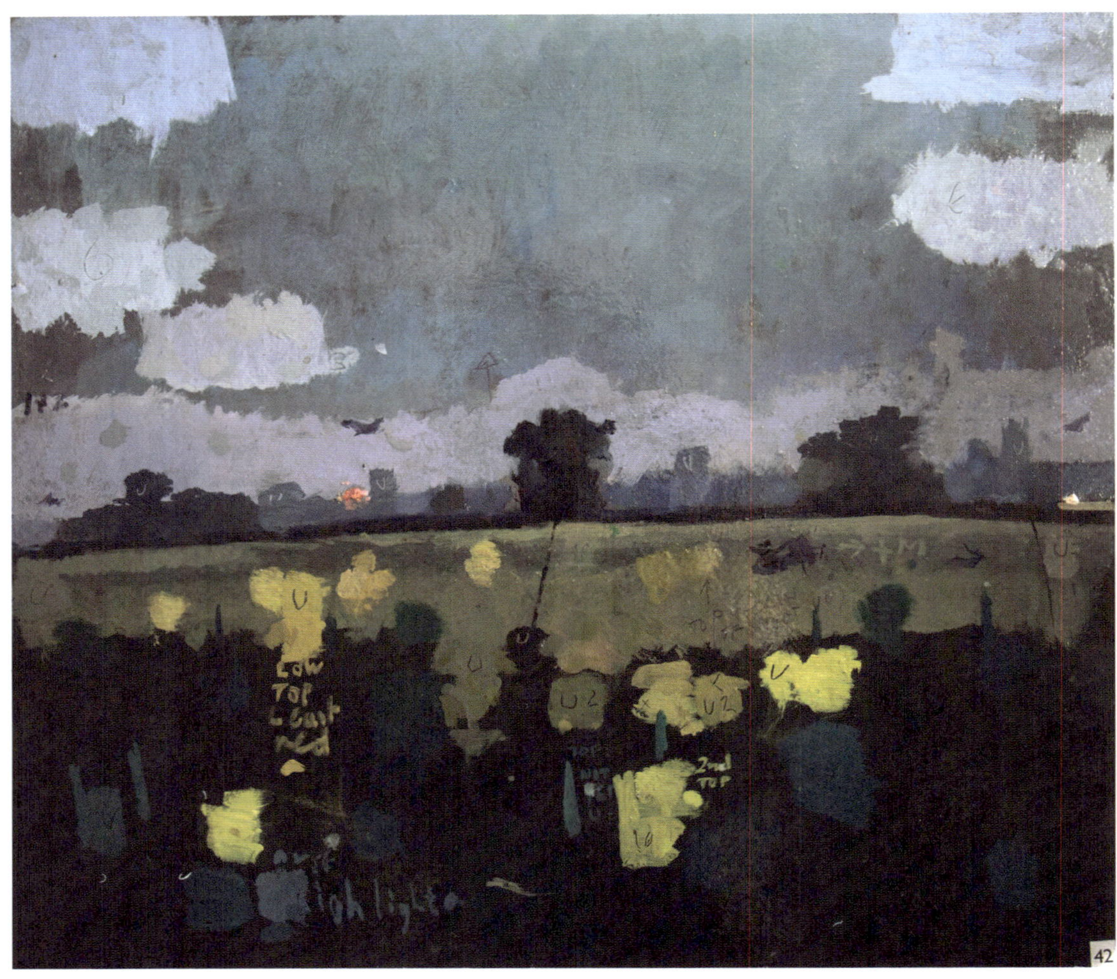

2 | Oil-on-board study with acrylic underpainting.
The clearly defined colour patches provide clear
values, like individual notes on a piano, for the
final painting.

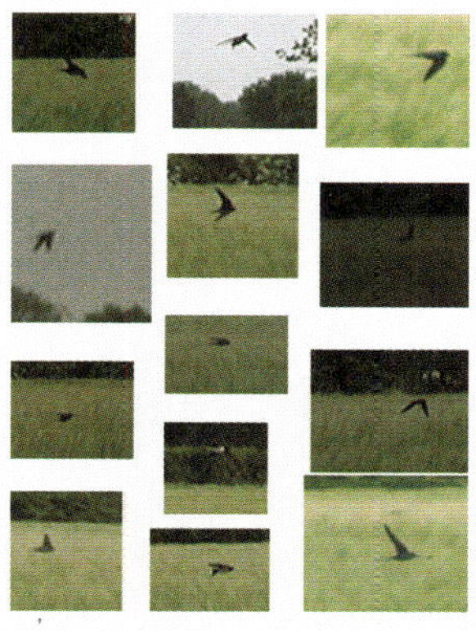

3 | I needed a visual source for swallows, so I went to a field of barley where I knew they hunted. I took some photos during the day that seemed to match what I'd seen at dusk in the rape field. I had to use bright light to get the speeds needed to capture such fast-moving objects.

painted some colours to record this, then noticed the crimson light of a radio mast in the distance and included that, as well as the cold yellow of the headlight of a passing car.

I packed up and went home. Figures 2 and 3

INDOORS

Computer Work

The next day my study looked both unfamiliar and somehow complete. These were both good signs. I transferred the photos into Adobe Photoshop to analyse as layers to help me discover the distribution of colours, a method that I first used to study colours in a field of corn.[2] Traditional oil painting also has layers: painters, like Titian, built images up from separate layers of colour, wet onto dry. This is the way I work. I use the colours from the study made outdoors to determine colours for the wet-on-dry layers that I build up on my painting in the studio.

The photos I took at the rape field were variously exposed for different parts of the scene. To find the distribution of a colour in the painted study, I first chose the photo that was best exposed to show that colour. I then used Photoshop's selection tool to pick out that colour in the photograph. Photoshop can then indicate every point in the photo where that colour appears. This breakdown reveals details not obvious to the naked eye and can clarify the scene in an unexpected way. I could now use this information to guide the distribution of paint of that colour onto the canvas. Only three photos were needed for this painting. Figures 4–9 After some trial and error, I could use this method to see the colour distributions in a way that would help me to read the scene more effectively.

The layers also revealed the colour distribution as a *texture gradient*, a regular increase in the number of texture elements proportional to the distance from the viewer. In experimental psychology, a texture gradient is a recognised depth cue. Since each texture is so closely associated with a colour, it seems more appropriate here to refer to them as *colour-textures*.[3]

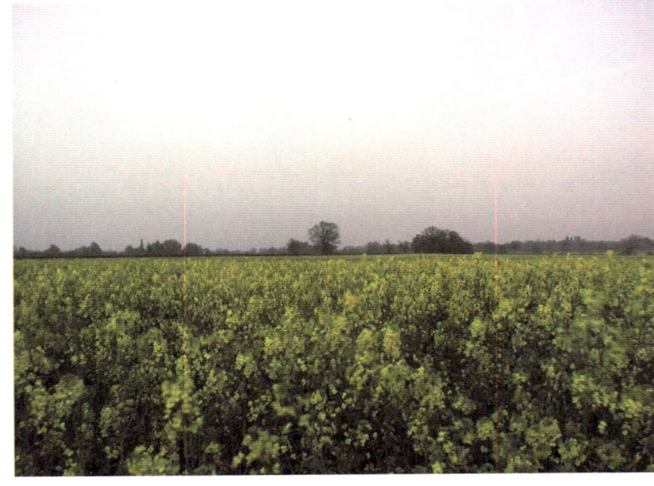

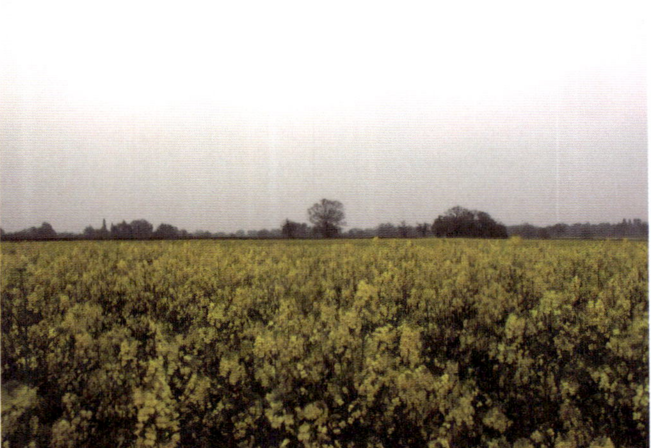

Clockwise from top left:
4 | Photograph showing the best exposure of the tonal range of sky that will match the range of the oil study
5 | Photograph exhibiting the best exposure of the distribution of yellows and greens
6 | Photograph showing an excellent range of tonal values in trees on the horizon

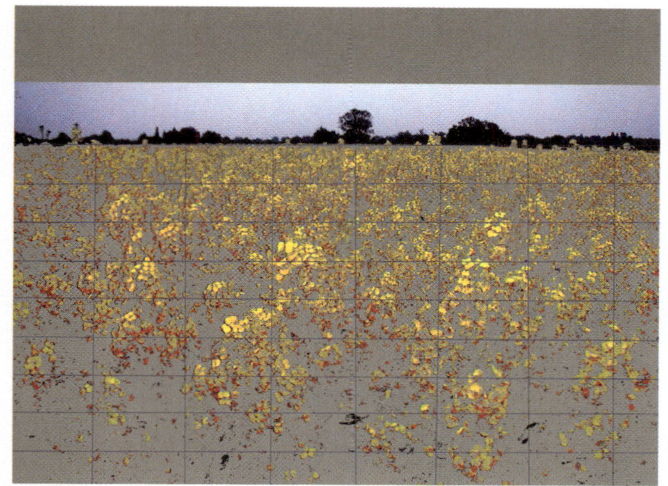

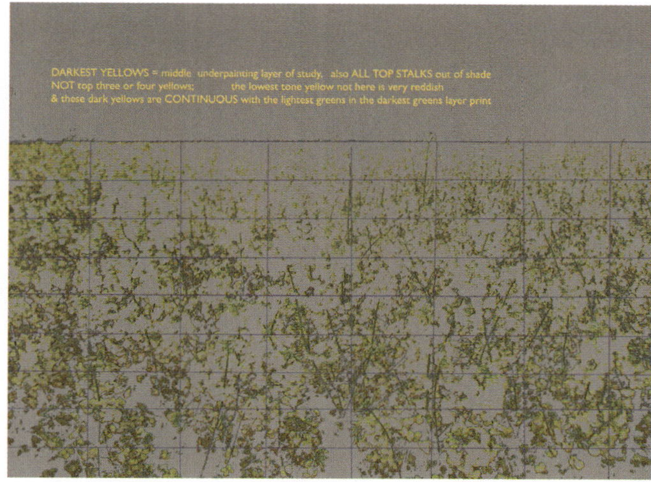

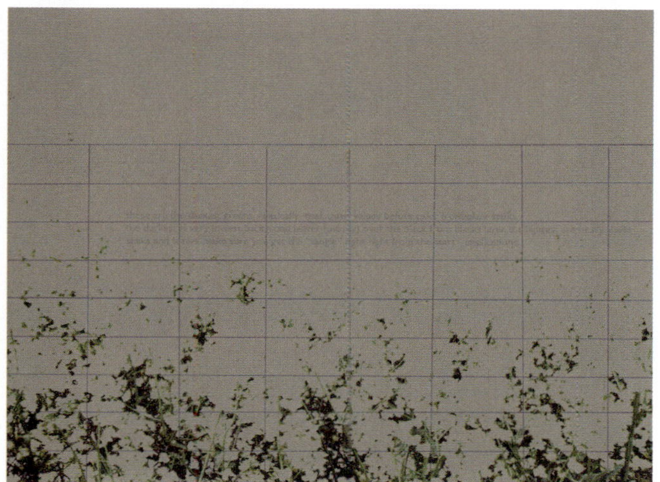

Clockwise from top left:

7 | This Photoshop selection layer picks out a range of yellows to show their distribution as a colour texture. (Some yellows have been switched red to make them easier to see.) The selection also reveals a texture gradient, a strong depth cue. A printout is used in the studio. Colours selected from the print are matched to corresponding colours of the oil study and are used to guide the distribution of the colours in the studio painting. The canvas has a grid to help transfer the distribution from print to painting.

8 | This Photoshop selection shows the distribution of the darkest yellows and greens. The actual colour mixes used in the painting will be the darkest yellows and greens from the oil study, but their distribution will be guided by a print of this image.

9 | Photoshop selection layer showing the distribution of the darkest greens and blacks

10 | A dark acrylic underpainting, originally for a night painting

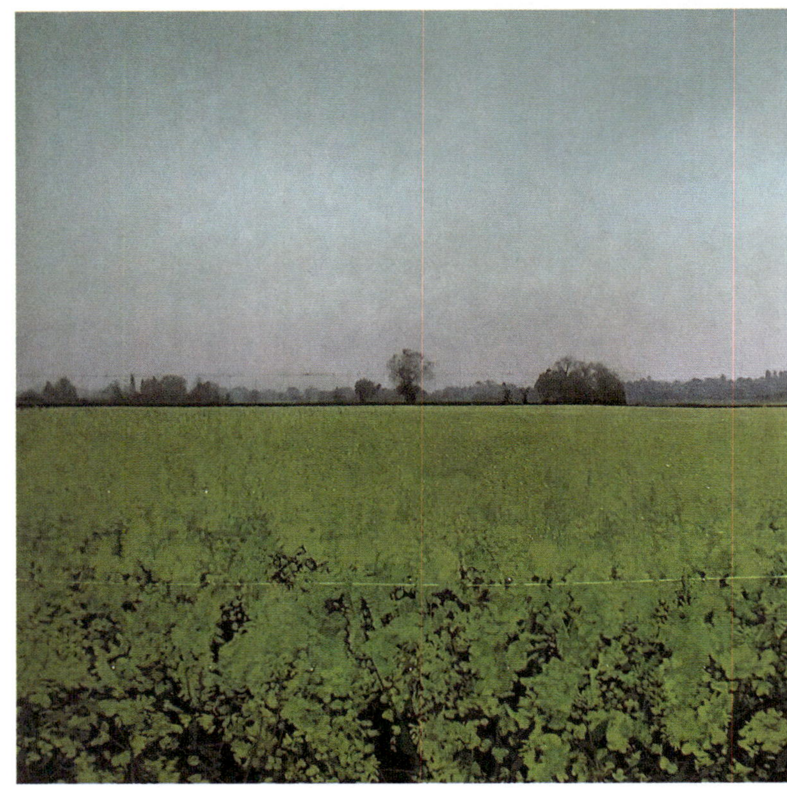

11 | Early transparent oil layers still affected by the dark underpainting. As the paint layers accumulate, light onto dark, the lighter colours will become increasingly opaque, producing an effect of paler solid objects above transparent, darker ones below. The piece of cotton running across the canvas is a part of a grid used to help transfer the colour distributions from the print out to the canvas.

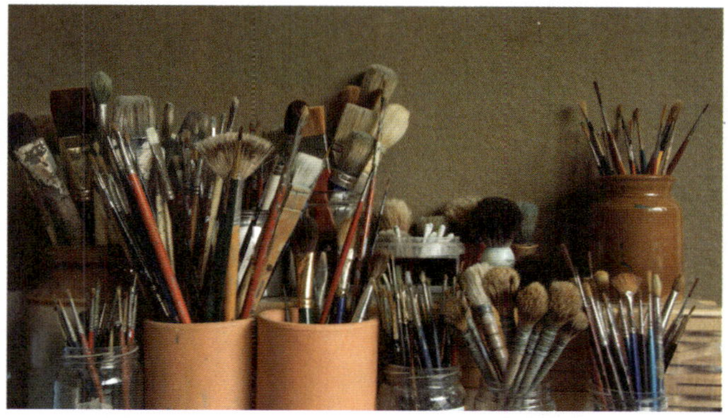

Some experimental psychologists are currently studying these types of association as an important new channel in visual processing. For me, they are a fundamental means with which human vision can disentangle or parse nature.

STUDIO PAINTING

I first had in mind a square painting, a night scene with the oak placed in the centre (to pair with an identically composed picture, *Swallows at 11am*, set in the morning). (See page 56.) This canvas had already been prepared with a dark acrylic underpainting. Figure 10 I decided to change the time of day of the scene but used this underpainting because the emotion I now wanted to express had a sense of floating on blackness about it.

After the painting was finished and I had compared it to its finished companion, *Swallows at 11am*, I decided to call the new painting *Swallows at 9pm*. Figures 11–16 The reference to the birds and to time suggests temporal scales at play. At least a year has passed between the two images, as evidenced by the crop rotation, rape following barley. The birds would have migrated to Africa and back. Of course the same 250-year-old oak remains; it offers a very different way of measuring time. There are only a few days in the year when the crop looks like this, only a few minutes in the day when light is like this, only a few seconds to see the birds.

In the ancient Roman world, bird watching was connected to augury. In the end there were four swallows, like little horsemen, and a tiny red light. I think this makes the beauty of the scene both uneasy and somehow more truthful.

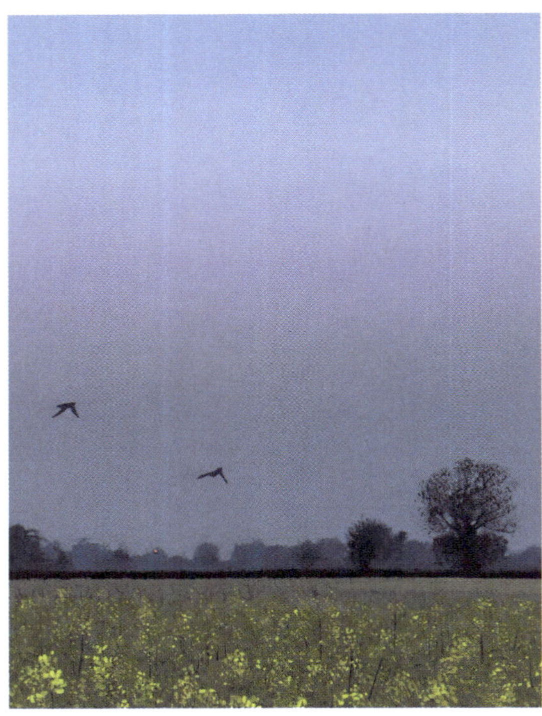

13, 14 | *Swallows at 9pm*, detail. There are differences in finish across a painting that brings out the character of the elements in it. These differences also reveal the artifice involved in the act of representation. The patterning of distinct layers is visible, and some white grid dots remain.

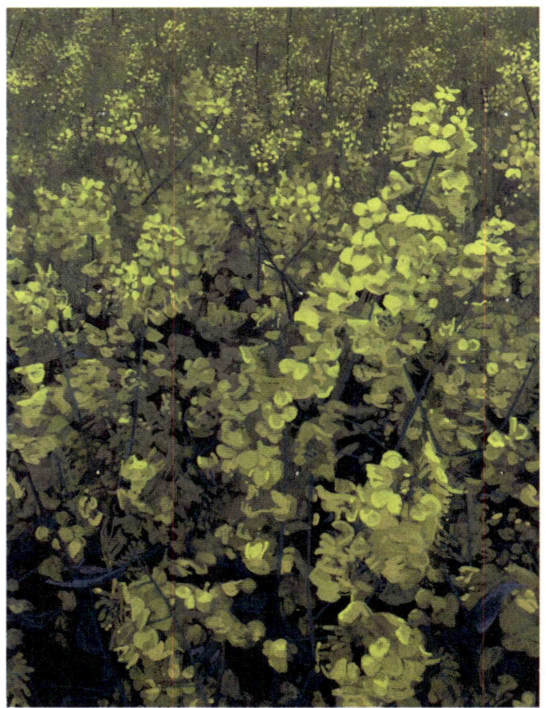

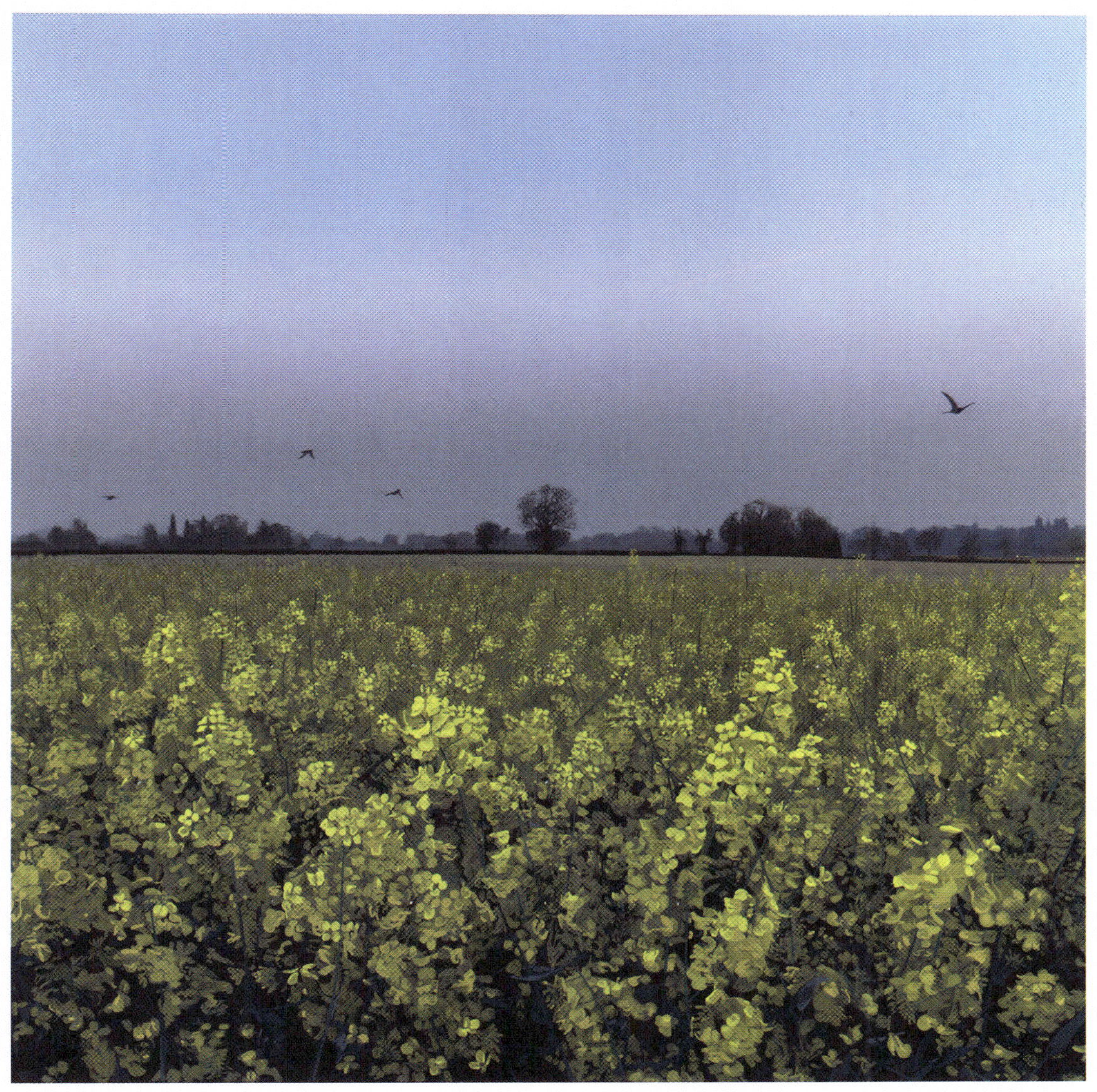

15 | *Swallows at 9pm*

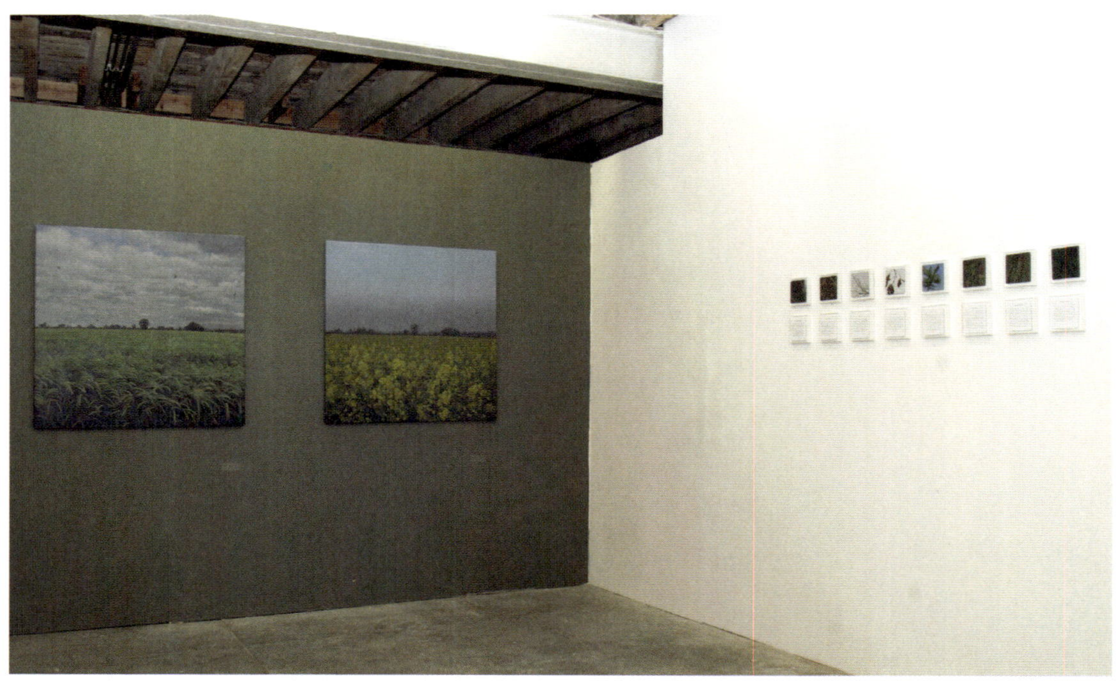

16 | *Swallows at 9pm* exhibited with *Swallows at 11am* and Semipermeable Membrane, at Vertigo, Shoreditch, London

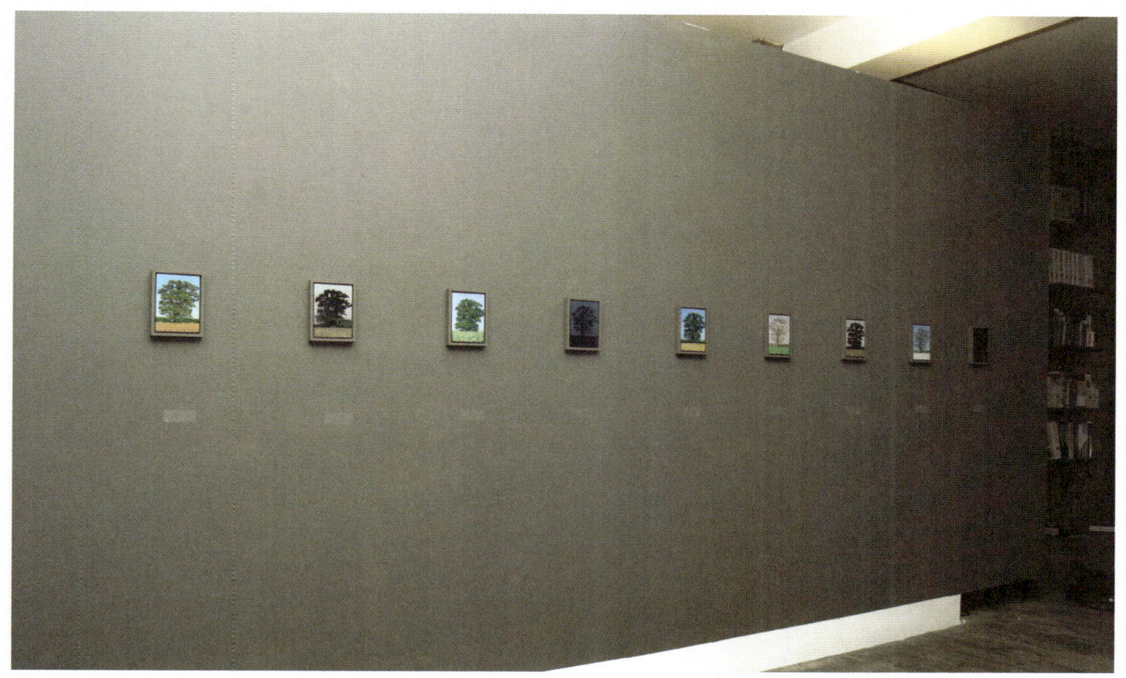

17 | A series of small oaks with grey frames on
a grey wall, suggesting small glass windows in a
chapel, at Vertigo

Conclusion:
Letting Nature Back into Painting

I see my work as an expression of a tradition that bridges popular and high arts and the interests of different generations. The making and display of paintings of place, especially places in nature that one feels an affinity for, has been widespread for centuries. But critical attention in the arts has for decades been focused elsewhere.

When I left university, I happily lectured art students on avant-garde modernism in all its forms—conceptual, formal, political—while ignoring the art on the walls of my own home. I felt no contradiction in that

I feel it now though. And in writing about my experiences as a painter of landscape, I am trying to correct this distortion in my own past and in cultural thinking. For I believe that observational landscape painting—nature painting—can be reclaimed as a modern art form.

Observational painting is familiar: many people paint such pictures at some time in their lives—at school or at home—or have a family member that does. One can thus sympathise with the activity by seeing it from the inside, as an attempt to make one's own form of contact with the subject. This shared practice provides the best possible seedbed for the renewal of an art.

The tradition I work in is broadly realist. It does not offer final descriptions of nature, any more than it claims that any one artist's personal vision is final. But it does offer tools for seeing and thinking about nature in new ways.

Constable described landscape painting as "this lovely art," and the pleasure that he took in painting nature is something that should speak directly to us today. His kind of realism—empirical, exploratory, taking pleasure in discovery—is a door we should open once again.[1] For nature painting as a shared practice could now be part of a much bigger enterprise. Because, to borrow the words of nature writer Robert Macfarlane, "a factually based but imaginatively driven restructuring of our relationship with nature is crucial for the future of us all."

Acknowledgments

I owe a lifelong debt to Alvyn Bates—painter and potter, and my first art teacher—whose craftsmanship and friendship still keeps my feet on the ground. I am also grateful for the teaching of professors T. J. Clark, who was at the Department of Fine Art at Leeds University during my time there, and the late Michael Podro and staff of the Department of Art History and Theory at Essex University, all of whom had a formative effect on my view of painting.

With help from John Jones at Leeds, Trevor Goodman and Tony Eggleston at Felsted School in Essex gave me my first opportunity to paint professionally. I also wish to remember Neil Kirk and Georgina James as well as to thank Amanda Brookes, who all helped me with kindness and patronage at times when it made a real difference to my career.

Ian Simpson and David Davies encouraged me while I was the head of the painting at the Open College of the Arts and opened my eyes to the important world of amateur painting. David, a musician and a former editor of the science journal *Nature*, edited the catalogue for the oak tree exhibition. I am also indebted to Catherine Shern of Vertigo for helping to conceive that show and bring the paintings to London.

Photographs of my artwork were provided by Prudence Cuming of London; additional photography by Sophie Dury. John Cupitt of Imperial College London adjusted the digital files for the panorama paintings on software of his own design and has been an inspiration with image processing in the studio. Thanks to the head teacher at Bhylls Acre Primary school in Wolverhampton for a new school cap; to Janet Spenser who compiled notes for Semipermeable Membrane; to Robert Macfarlane for permission to quote from his email; and to Ken Adlard, of New Moon Photography in Norfolk, who took the time to photograph me and the tree. The installation shots are by Iain Lowe.

Two conversations in particular helped me understand what I do a little more deeply. Jules Pretty, of the Department of Biological Sciences at the University of Essex, connected my painting to other cultures that use landscape stories to link shared meaning to a sense of place. John Mollon, fellow at Gonville and Caius College in Cambridge, introduced me to the scientific association between colour and texture in visual processing. John coined the phrase "parsing nature" to describe my work.

My debt to Alain de Botton is considerable. Not only did he contribute a foreword here, his book *The Pleasures and Sorrows of Work* brought my paintings to the attention of a global public. I also count him as a friend.

The farm where the oak still grows belonged to Peter and Gillian Spenser. I will always be grateful to them and to Bill Jack and Reg Cockle, who worked there, for their help and kindness over the seven years.

A big thank you to my publisher, Kevin Lippert, for imagining *Oak* in the first place, and to my editors, Jennifer Lippert and Linda Lee, for their patient, professional help at every stage. Thank you to Bree Anne Apperley for her thoughtful and beautiful design work. And, finally, thanks to Stephen and Sue Kerridge, who provided the perfect bolt-hole on their fenland farm, where this book was written.

Notes

Introduction

1. One book, *Light and Colour in the Outdoors,* trans. L. Seymour (New York: Springer Verlag, 1993) by Belgian astronomer M. G. J. Minnaert, in particular opened my eyes. The author explains the physics of natural phenomena in a relatively nontechnical way. There is information on the colour of puddles, the scattering of light by clouds, the factors that make the blues in the sky change in the way they do—hundreds of effects are described. The book is a catalogue of fresh starting points for new nature painting. I now keep a copy in my car.

Process

1. Most of the colours we see every day have two components: the colour of the object itself and the colour of the light falling on that object. If a painter mixes observed colours correctly, as the colours accumulate across the picture, the eye is able to sense illumination—common to all the colours—as light falling on the objects, specific to that time and place. Creating daylight and moonlight in this way is one of the great pleasures of landscape painting.

2. Computer software offers many new ways for visual artists to work with visual information. For example, for *Swallows at 9pm* I worked with three separate exposures, one digital file for each of three brightness levels in the landscape. But new software now makes it possible to combine several differently exposed shots into *one* image, with almost every area correctly exposed. This is called high dynamic range or (HDR) imagery. I am currently experimenting with HDR photos as source images for new paintings.

3. I first found texture gradients described in David Marr's *Vision: A Computational Investigation into the Human Representation and Processing of Visual Information* (New York: W.H. Freeman and Company, 1982). Marr describes a wide range of visual-grouping effects useful for artists.

Conclusion

1. The empirical tradition in British arts has often come into contact with British science. The relationship has been particularly fruitful in the area of perception. How this interaction between science and art could transform the way nature is seen is described by Richard Holmes in his book *The Age of Wonder: How the Romantic Generation Discovered the Beauty and Terror of Science* (London: Harper Press, 2008).

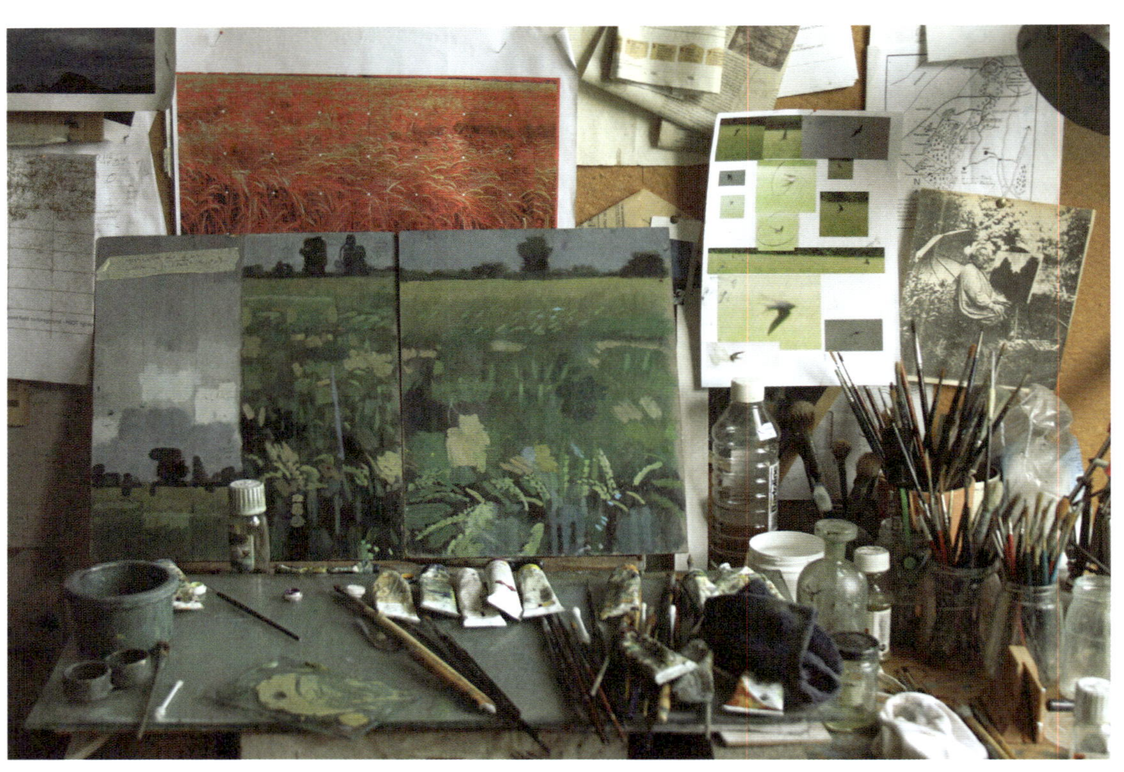